CAT FRIENDS, BOTH FERAL AND DOMESTIC

CAT FRIENDS, BOTH FERAL AND DOMESTIC

A book for current and prospective cat people

JENNIFER L. JOHNSON

First Printing, 2023

for my Mom
and also all of our cats,
who, unfortunately, cannot read
but who surely appreciate the fact that
I have written a book about them

Contents

I

Opening Remarks

"What have you been doing lately?" my 15-year-old niece asked me. "Seems like you've been busy at home on the computer a lot."

"Yep! I've been working more hours than usual online," I explained. "And in my free time, I'm writing a book."

She looked surprised. "You're writing a book?"

"Well, yes," I replied.

She narrowed her eyes and looked at me seriously. "Is it about cats?" she asked.

"Yes," I confirmed. "It is indeed about cats."

"Oh, okay," she responded. She no longer looked surprised.

I suppose I have become a stereotypical cat lady. I currently have six indoor cats and six outdoor cats. I love them.

I'm not sure who my target audience is here. Along with my reflections on the nature of cats and the meaning of life, I've included true stories about specific feral and domesticated cats and tips that may help people who want to understand cats better or who simply want to join me in admiring them and contemplating how best to serve their needs. I am not a veterinarian, and I don't pretend to have expertise in feline biology or psychology. I merely offer my own insight.

And insight into the workings of the natural world may, I fear, be in short supply these days – at least judging from social media. In early 2023, I saw a two-part story on Facebook that led me to realize just how many people walk among us with no understanding of animals. In the first part of the story, a woman sees a cat with its head stuck in a fence, helps it get loose, determines that it is completely uninjured, brings it into her house, takes photos of it, and then posts about it on a neighborhood site hoping to find its owner, noting that it is "very mean and pees on everything" but has not scratched or bitten her. This post immediately receives a number of comments from people informing the woman that the cat in the photos is a wild bobcat. In the second part of the story, the woman creates a follow-up post saying "Oh silly me! Everybody look what I did! I brought a wild bobcat into my house thinking it was someone's cat! Well, how was I supposed to know? I didn't grow up in this area so I didn't know what a bobcat looks like!"

This post received thousands of comments, most of which either praised her for her act of kindness, scolded her for doing something so foolish, or defended her against the people saying that she had acted foolishly. I was shocked by how few comments there were questioning the validity of this obviously fake story. I assume it was either a photoshop job or a photo of somebody's domesticated wildcat raised in captivity. I did some quick digging online and found that the same story had been posted on Twitter in 2019, and the same thing had happened in the comments – people mostly praised or blamed the woman for bringing a bobcat inside. Where were all of the comments asking for more details? Why didn't the bobcat run off at the speed of light once she released its head from the fence? Since it was apparently not injured, stunned, in shock, or unconscious, how did she manage to carry it into her house? Once inside her house with the door closed, why did the bobcat not explode and start literally bouncing off of the walls? I once trapped a 7-year-old, heavily pregnant feral cat who was somewhat accustomed to people, and when I gently opened the cage door and released her into a small, carpeted bedroom, she instantly went berserk. She tried to leap to the top of the walls, probably thinking that she might be able to get up and out of the room, and she leapt so high that her front paws actually touched the ceiling. I simply cannot believe that a person could pick up a wildcat, carry it into a house, close the door, and set it down without sustaining 911-type injuries. So my comment on the Facebook post was, "Here's the world's least necessary piece of advice: Don't pick up an uninjured adult bobcat and bring it inside your house. It's unnecessary advice because nobody would be able to do it even if they were foolish enough to try."

Like the gullible commenters on the Facebook page, we may all be tempted to underestimate the athletic prowess of the humble house cat and forget for a moment that cats are our superiors in so many ways. If we had their power in proportion to our height, we could bend our knees slightly and then spring to a 4th-floor balcony. As it is, I'm afraid we can't even follow them to the top of the refrigerator without something to give us a boost.

2

Yearbook Photos

The following is the cast of characters who have inspired this book and who will feature prominently throughout it. I've used their 2023 yearbook photos and separated them into three groups: my indoor cats, my outdoor cats, and my mom's indoor cats. You might notice some family resemblances. Bright Eyes, Beauty, and Cassie are sisters, Clouseau is their nephew, and all of the outdoor cats, along with Shadow and Miss Marple, share some ancestors.

By the way, this book contains a variety of formats and doesn't really have to be read in order, so if you get bored with one chapter, you can just skip to the next one and see if you like it better.

INDOOR FRIENDS

Athena, *high jump state champion; Debate Club President*

Chloe, *President of the Welcoming Committee*

Claude, *voted most likely to get whatever he wants*

Cleopatra, *Drama Club President*

Clouseau, *Chariman of the Complaints Department*

Lionel, *voted most likely to become a model or end up in jail*

OUTDOOR FRIENDS

Beauty, *voted least likely to participate in a group project*

Cassie, *voted most skeptical*

Duchess, *voted most elusive*

Martha, *President of Community Outreach*

Princess, *President of the Mean Girls Club*

Sibling, *voted best all-around male athlete*

MOM'S FRIENDS

Bright Eyes, *voted most loyal*

Claudia, *voted most full of surprises*

Miss Marple, *voted least likely to miss a meal*

Peppermint, *Chairman of Event Planning Committee*

Shadow, *voted most likely to lie around on his back all day*

Extracurriculars are fun! Clockwise from top: an assembly of the Bug-Watchers Club; a Bug-Catchers activity; a Birdwatchers Club session; a meeting of the Interior Decorators Club

3

F. A. Q.

Q: How can I interpret tail position to tell what mood a cat is in?

A: Straight up in the air means the cat is in a good mood, feeling positive, feeling confident, willing to be sociable. Straight up with a little curl at the tip or a "question mark" appearance means the cat is extra happy and very interested in friendly social interaction (either with you or with a nearby cat). Tail straight back from the body horizontally usually means the cat is checking out the situation, not scared but not entirely confident either. Tail low and pointed to the ground indicates fear, nervousness, or a very cautious attitude. Tail tucked means fearful and submissive. A twitching or thrashing tail means the cat is annoyed or about to attack someone or something (or is at least considering it). Most exciting of all, a vertical tail with tail spasms reveals joy.

Q: What does it mean if my cat's tail is in a neutral or downward position and then shoots straight up when she sees me?

A: Lucky you! Your cat is very happy to see you.

Q: Should I make it my goal in life to create such a happy and safe environment that my cats will start each day in a good mood, appearing at breakfast time with their tails straight up in the air?

A: Yes.

Q: Sometimes my cat flicks her upright tail back and forth against my leg like she is petting me with her tail. Sometimes she curls her tail around my lower leg. What does this behavior indicate?

A: Your cat loves you! You are lucky to live with a cat who appreciates you so much!

Q: How about a floofy tail? What does it mean?

A: It means the cat is very scared. It usually happens quite suddenly as a result of a surge of adrenaline in response to fear. It is often accompanied by an arched back and floofy or standing-up-straight fur along the spine. Kittens react in this manner to make themselves appear less vulnerable. I'm not a tiny kitten! I'm a floofy wolf! You should be scared of me!

Q: Floofy tails are hilarious! Can I scare my cat on purpose to make him arch and floof?

A: That's mean. Think about how you feel when you just barely avoid a car accident. The sudden surge of adrenaline and racing heart do not make you feel good at all.

Q: What other cat signals can I interpret?

A: If a cat looks you in the eye and blinks slowly, it means she likes and trusts you. You should return the slow blink. You can also initiate slow blinks if you are trying to gain a cat's trust. If a cat slowly blinks, arches, and offers you her forehead to bump or pet, that's a very affectionate gesture.

Q: What can I tell from looking at a cat's eyes?

A: Cats' pupils dilate in low light and constrict in bright light, just like people's. If lighting conditions are normal and a cat's pupils are dilated, it generally means that the cat is scared, angry, stressed, on high alert, or about to attack. With a friendly indoor cat, pupils will dilate during play sessions as the cat pounces on toys. With feral cats, pupils usually dilate because of stress. If your indoor cat's pupils are always dilated, even when you shine a light toward them, it could mean that the cat has a medical problem such as diabetes and should be checked out by a vet.

Q: Why does my cat bite me?

A: Cats sometimes give social bites that are really more like "mouthing with teeth" than biting. If the cat puts his or her teeth on your flesh in a biting move but doesn't bite down hard and doesn't quickly move away, that's a social bite. If, on the other hand, the cat bites you hard and then quickly jerks his head away, all in an instant, then you have been bitten for real by a cat who is probably temporarily angry at you or fearful of you (and you might have deserved it). Sometimes cats bite in an act of "redirected aggression," as a way of expressing anger, frustration, fear, or sadness caused by someone or something other than the bite victim. For example, if a cat has been rejected by another cat or person, he will be full of difficult emotions and may bite the next person he sees. Another type of biting can occur when cats become overstimulated during play or petting and just bite in response. You can usually sense that this is about to happen if you observe the tail motions. Personally, I can relate to "overstimulation biting" because I usually clench my jaw and/or grind my teeth while interacting with cats who are being cute. I suppose the cuteness sensors in my brain become overloaded, which for some reason then activates the muscles in my jaw.

Q: Why does my kitten bite me?

A: It's a kitten. Kittens bite. They are developing their cat skills. If you don't like the biting, don't put your hand on the kitten's belly. If the kitten attacks you and bites, redirect the biting behavior to a kitten-safe toy. Don't try to discipline the kitten because (1) that's mean and (2) it won't work. Just redirect.

Q: My kitten suckles on me - on my neck, my hand, my arm, or my clothes or blanket. Is this normal? Will suckling persist into adulthood?

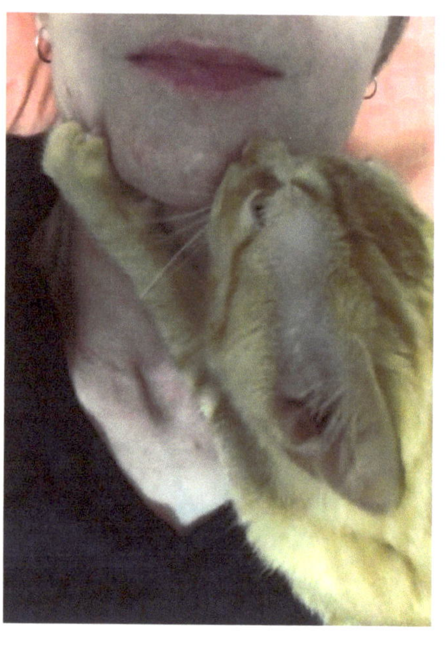

A: It's not really the norm, but it's not uncommon either. Kittens have a strong suckling impulse, of course, and if they are separated from their mother before the age of about eight to ten weeks, they will likely continue to suckle for a while. My Athena suckled vigorously once or twice per day until she was about five months old and then slowly decreased frequency until she was only suckling once in a while if she felt particularly affectionate or vulnerable. She stopped suckling completely around the age of one and a half years. Lionel suckled my neck and face a lot as a little guy and didn't stop until he was almost two years old. My other cats never suckled on me at all. My mom's Bright Eyes has always suckled on blankets, even as an adult.

Q: Do cats like routines?

A: Yes.

Q: Anything I should know about feeding routines?

A: I think most people assume that cats don't care about things like dishes, but some of them might. If the dish or plate is too lightweight, it irritates them because it moves around as they try to eat. If it's too small, it annoys them because there's no room for their whiskers. If a cat has a big head and long whiskers (like my Lionel and Clouseau), he needs a big wide bowl or heavy plate. It's important to let kittens and young cats graduate to grown-up cat dishware as they get bigger; kitten dishes are just too small for adult cats. As for the type of food, it's best to take advice from your veterinarian. Personally, I feed both wet and dry food. I stay away from the cheapest dry food because it might just be low-quality grains sprayed with meat-flavored oils, but I can't afford the most expensive stuff either. I usually buy Purina One dry food products and Fancy Feast canned foods. Royal Canin is my favorite for underweight kittens; I use the Mother and Baby Cat canned pate, then transition to the dry baby cat kibble, then to the dry kitten food, and then eventually off of the Royal Canin line since it is too expensive for me to make it a daily cat food.

Q: Why does it sometimes seem like my cat wants me to stay with her while she eats?

A: She trusts you to have her back and defend her if any threat emerges suddenly while she is focusing on her food. Generally, this behavior indicates that she loves her person and that she is perhaps not 100% confident in the safety of the environment. If there's any unusual activity in the house (like men working on something), my Athena will not eat at all unless I sit right next to her while she eats.

Q: What about litter? Any advice?

A: Not really. I have yet to find the perfect litter and have had problems with every type of litter I've tried. I love the natural grass type because it does not create dust and it lasts a really long time, but it tracks all over the place and it does not mask smells. I like the clumping clay variety for its odor control and manageable amount of tracking, but it creates too much dust for my liking. Even the so-called 99% dust-free clay-based varieties seem to create clouds of dust, so I question the veracity of the claim. The new wood-product based litter did not please me at all, as it created loads of dust both in the air and on the cats' paws, and my cats hated it. In fact, one of my cats hated it so much that she started peeing in the sink. I tried a few other clay alternatives, but the cats did not like them. At first, we liked the old-newspaper-based pellet variety, but it doesn't last long for adults, and kittens tend to eat it. For kittens, it's important to use non-clumping litter because they are likely to try eating some of it, and clumping litter could expand in the digestive system and kill them.

Q: Do I really have to have one litter box per cat (or one box plus one extra for each cat, as Jackson Galaxy says)?

A: For multi-cat households, it's important to have enough litter boxes for everyone and to keep them clean, but I don't think that everyone needs one. I have five boxes in my house for six cats. I really don't want more. I could probably downsize to four.

Q: Do indoor cats in a multi-cat household like to use each other's litterboxes?

A: Yes. They may even sneak into each other's rooms to use the litterbox. It's partly a dominant behavior and perhaps partly a desire to keep their own areas clean.

Q: Why is my cat defiant? Is he disobeying me on purpose?

A: Your cat has his own will and likes to express it, just like a kid does (or an adult, for that matter). And just as a kid gets upset with a parent who tries to rein in his activities, a cat will challenge the authority of a person who tries to prevent him from exercising his free will. So, yes, your cat might be disobeying you on purpose as a way to maintain his sense of agency. He might also be the victim of bad or confusing communication. In any case, the problem is more likely to be you than him. Responding to his defiance with anger or more defiance will not yield good results.

Q: Are cats more dramatic than people?

A: They can be, especially during thunderstorms. It only takes one cat to set off a chain reaction of leaping and crashing. During a recent storm when we were all sitting in the living room together, there was a clap of thunder so loud that it caused Athena to fly straight up into the air and then land on top of Lionel, who then, more startled by Athena than by the storm, sprang straight up in the air and landed on Claude, creating a tangle of three cats that then exploded again into the air. Lionel ran in a panic toward the kitchen and slammed into the trash can while Athena and Claude flew above him onto the counter and then onto the top of the refrigerator. In the meantime, Clouseau had knocked over a chair, sending Cleopatra and Chloe under the couch.

Q: Is there anything more ridiculous than a cat trying to run at high speed around a corner on a laminate floor?

A: Not that I know of.

Q: Do cats get FOMO (Fear of Missing Out)?

A: Yes. In fact, no creature on Earth gets as bad a case of FOMO as a kitten whose littermate has food, especially sloppy wet "gruel" (a mixture of canned kitten food and kitten formula). Even if the kitten has its own food, it will still get FOMO. As a way of expressing this FOMO, the kitten will plunge its entire body into the littermate's food. Adult cats may also get FOMO, but more often regarding affection than food. If a cat who enjoys human attention suspects that another cat somewhere is being petted or cuddled, then the first cat will suffer from FOMO and may act out with sulking, meowing, yowling, or acting aggressively toward the cat that's getting the attention.

Q: Can cats feel empathy or sympathy for other creatures?

A: Yes, but generally only for members of the same species and those above them on the food chain, not below. Cats can show sympathy for cats, dogs, people, and perhaps some other creatures but never for any critter that might be prey. Historically, this same principle has held true for humans, who have shown no sympathy for the people who are considered in any way beneath them (below them on the food chain due to social, economic, racial, or national factors).

Q: Are cats really loners at heart or do they like to share their experiences with others?

A: Some cats are introverts and some are extroverts, but most cats do seem to appreciate sharing their interests with other cats or people. My indoor cats get happy when I join them in looking out the window at birds, just like we humans enjoy watching an especially funny or good TV show with friends and family. The cats watch the birds or squirrels, cackle, then look at me and head-bump me or even walk around me and then resume looking out the window. It's more fun watching with a friend.

Q: Do individual cats' personalities change over time?

A: Not really, unless they become grumpier, meaner, or more wary, distrustful, and anxious due to bad or traumatic experiences. In other words, the same answer as for people.

Q: How long does it take a person to gain the trust of a feral cat?

A: It could take years.

Q: Is it worth it?

A: Yes, of course.

Q: Can cats be trained to overcome their impulses and modify their behavior?

A: Maybe. Can you overcome your impulses? Can you modify your behavior? Oh, you can? Then why don't you? I recently told my mom that I didn't want to take home the bag of Doritos she was trying to give me because I was afraid I would eat the whole bag and then feel sick. "Well, just eat a few at a time, then, silly!" Thanks, Mom. Good advice.

Q: Are cat communities socialist or capitalist?

A: This one is tricky. Cats lean more socialist than capitalist, but they don't believe that the world could be made fair if only they turned over all resources to a central governing body and empowered that body to distribute all needed goods equally. They certainly don't want every aspect of their lives controlled by a central power. However, they do seem more capable than people of abiding by the famous principle: "from each according to his ability, to each according to his need." Cats will hunt alone or together (each according to his or her ability) and then share the kill with other members of the community, even allowing the largest males to eat first and eat the most (each according to his need). They may also raise kittens together and care for sick and injured community members by making food available to them. They share their spaces with each other and have at least some sense of community spirit. They are pro-private property, though, and they discriminate against strangers, both of which conflict with their socialist leanings. Many of them will keep resources to themselves, and all of them appreciate the freedom to make individual choices like good capitalists.

Q: Are cats more liberal, conservative, or moderate? Would they vote Democrat or Republican?

A: Most cats would probably be categorized as political moderates since they are unlikely to be either far left-wing or far right-wing. While they oppose government overreach, they also refrain from supporting overly ambitious enterprises designed to create enormous wealth. Cats do not support the Democrats or the Republicans, and they remain superior to petty politicking.

Q: Are cats competitive?

A: All animals are competitive to some extent. In fact, plants are also competitive. Maybe plants are even more competitive than animals. It's always the quiet ones.

Q: So will the honeysuckle eventually kill all of the grass in my back yard?

A: I hope so. I hate mowing, and the cats love the honeysuckle because it creates shaded hiding places.

The cats are not in their houses -- they're under the honeysuckle

2021

2022

2023
chair has been
eaten by
honeysuckle

Q: Do I need to worry about toxic plants in my yard?

A: Reasonable caution is advised. The ASPCA's list of toxic plants is available online.

Q: Do cats recognize a binary gender-role system?

A: Yes. Especially in feral cat colonies, male and female gender roles seem to be recognized.

Q: Do male cats or female cats make better pets?

A: Bottom line: cats are individuals, and behavior and personality cannot be predicted based on gender alone. I have often found males to be more cuddly and affectionate than females, but there are certainly plenty of female cuddlebugs. Males can also be more aggressive and territorial, and there is more potential for serious fighting among cats in a household or yard if males are involved, even if they are neutered. In my experience, female cats may squabble with other female cats and even chase each other, but they are less likely to become a fighting ball of cat, rolling around all teeth and claws. I have known female cats who absolutely, positively hate all other cats, though, so perhaps the girls *could* end up in a fighting ball of cat if the opportunity presented itself. People who want to have multiple cats will have an easier time if they adopt same-age kittens who can learn how to play and fight each other safely.

Q: Do cats discriminate against people on the basis of gender, race, age, sexual orientation, religion, ethnicity, or income level?

A: No, but some cats might be guilty of stereotyping based on size or gender. If a big man is mean to them, they might then be fearful of all big men. If a toddler tortures them, they might then be afraid of all little kids.

Q: Do cats know if a person is good or bad?

A: Yes.

Q: How do material circumstances affect behavior?

A: Same as with people. If your environment is safe and you find plenty of food, water, and shelter every day without having to work for it, the various aspects of your true personality will emerge, and you will tend to trust others more easily. If you live in a survival situation from day to day, you will remain wary and distrustful, and the extreme tendencies of your personality will manifest more often because of your vulnerability. Your coping strategies will magnify themselves and dominate your whole personality.

Q: Who would win one of those "spot the difference" games – a cat or a person?

A: A cat would win if the game were played in real life – for instance, if you had a "before" and "after" room or two rooms side by side. I suppose a person would always win an image-based game.

Q: Can cats tell time?

A: Yes.

Q: Can cats count?

A: Yes. If I give four treats several days in a row and then give three, Athena will look at me and look around for the fourth one, as if to say, can't you count? That was three. There should be four.

Q: Do cats understand more words than you think they do?

A: Yes.

Q: Can cats read?

A: No.

Q: How will cats use technology in the future?

A: As AI improves, cats will have access to more tools that help them communicate in ways that humans can readily understand. An AI-powered machine could "read" their body language and "listen" to their meows and then translate what they are saying to their people, or the machine could simply provide what is needed directly (food, water, petting, treats, toys). Cat paw pads already work on touch-screens, and there are already smartphone apps for cats. The software will improve as thousands more computer science graduates look for things to do.

Q: Will advances in AI technology put the typical cat and the typical human on more equal footing?

A: Yes. In the frighteningly near future, even in the most modernized countries, the masses of people will be illiterate. Whenever written text is required, the people will speak to a computer that will write for them, and they will have the computer read text to them. Only the most educated elite will be able to read and write for themselves. The people will not feel sad or underprivileged about being illiterate any more than kids today feel sad about not being able to read a road map or do simple math operations without a calculator. With the skill of reading and writing obsolete, the masses of people will then be even more easily controlled by those in power than they are today. In the meantime, cats will also be using technology, but it will increase their power rather than taking it away. Hence, cats will rise as people fall.

Q: Will cats start using social media for themselves?

A: Of course not. While many people obsessively cultivate an online presence to manipulate others' perception of them, cats simply have no interest in creating or maintaining a personal image or brand. Cats are fully conscious beings with an awareness of themselves and others, but they are not self-conscious in the way that people are; cats do not concern themselves with the issue of how others view them. They are who they are, they know who they are, and they do not particularly care what others think of their appearance, personality, or accomplishments.

Q: Why do so many women become crazy cat ladies as they get older?

A: As people age, they tend to become somewhat more like cats as they grow more comfortable with their own life choices and care less about what others think of them. Hence, they may feel a greater affinity for cats, sensing a stronger connection with and appreciation for cats' individuality and cats' rejection of socially motivated fakery. Moreover, cats make great friends and, although they have a reputation for being judgemental, they actually not only tolerate but willingly accept their people's personality quirks and behaviors.

Q: Do cats remember their kittenhood?

A: Yes, I would guess that their memories go back to the age of about 8 - 10 weeks. Just like people, they seem nostalgic for toys, routines, and activities that they enjoyed as kittens. You can tell by the purring and the dreamy look that crosses their faces, and no, I don't think it's because they just like that toy or activity. Why does Lionel always purr when we snuggle in his favorite spot in his bedroom, where he spent all of his time as a kitten, but not when we snuggle on the couch? Why does Clouseau want to knead and purr in my lap right before bedtime just like he always did with his first mom? They might not understand why, but they are probably reconnecting with their inner kitten to experience the sensation of seeking and finding comfort.

Q: Can I make my outdoor cats stop killing birds, bugs, snakes, mice, etc.?

A: Probably not, unless you're the kind of person who can make a teenage boy stop playing video games or a teenage girl stop looking at her phone, in which case I suppose anything is possible.

Q: After human beings become extinct, will cats still roam the planet?

A: Quite possibly.

4

Personalities

"Other cats don't really have personalities," an acquaintance of mine once declared as he introduced me to his three cats. "But these three, my gosh! They really do! Each one has his own distinctive character. I don't like other people's cats because, you know, they're boring. But I couldn't live without these guys."

Of course I smiled and told him how great his cats seemed. I appreciated his love for them. At the same time, though, my inner cat was judging this man harshly. He was a psychologist, for crying out loud, and had concluded from his own experiences that his cats were unique in their uniqueness and that all other cats were just generic, four-legged creatures with no interesting qualities. His absurd lack of understanding amused me.

Any real cat lover knows that cats have personalities just as much as people do. To those who argue that there aren't as many variations in personality types among cats as there are among people, I would like to point out that they may be overestimating the complexity of people. They might then argue that cats are predictable. Sure they are. Aren't people? Most of the actions and reactions of living beings on our planet are entirely foreseeable. An individual member of a species may defy expectation, but, taken as a whole, the species remains predictable.

Recent documentaries, books, and studies about cats have put forth new categories of cat personalities. I find these interesting but not entirely satisfying. Some of them are based too heavily on the cat's interaction with their one special human friend. Would you want an assessment of your personality to be based on how you interact with just one person?

Overly scientific explanations for cat behavior also really bother me. Why do cats rub their faces against other cats or people? "Scientists" say that cats are simply marking territory with their pheromones as a way to claim possession and make it easier to identify community members and personal property. While it may be true that cats can locate their friends, loved ones, and favorite wall corners by scent, it is certainly also true that cats feel and express affection and experience emotions. The "scientists" say that animal "love" can be explained by the purely instinctive drive to reproduce and pass on DNA (unlike human beings, who, as a species, *aren't* driven by any instinctive drives, I suppose). According to this line of thinking, the emotions of animals are not as significant as the emotions of people (and the emotions of poor people and enslaved people were not as significant as the emotions of non-poor, non-enslaved people). To be fair, we should try turning the tables and see how it sounds.

Here, two human beings kiss as a way to decide if they will mate and produce offspring. If the woman detects MHC genes that are sufficiently different from hers, she will want to accept the man as her mate, since a diversity of genetic elements is likely to result in a stronger immune system in the offspring and, hence, a greater chance of propagating her DNA.

Here, a female human being tries to attract a dominant male human being. She is instinctively drawn to this type of male since he will likely have the strength to protect her offspring and defend them from predators, ensuring the survival of her line of DNA.

Here, a middle-aged male human being courts a younger female human being. Her youth makes her an excellent candidate for mating, since she will have enough time and energy to bear him many offspring, ensuring the survival of his line of DNA.

Here, a human male father protects his offspring to ensure the survival of his line of DNA.

These cats love each other and like to spend time together. They would be sad if they were parted.

This cat loves this person and enjoys spending time with her. The cat knows if the person needs extra love or comfort and is happy to offer it.

In this image, a mother cat enjoys being with her adorable kitten.

Factors affecting feral vs. domestic personalities

Material circumstances will impact the personality development and behavior of both cats and people. Creatures that grow up in situations where their survival is constantly at risk will behave differently and relate differently to others than will creatures that grow up in safe environments where all needs are met without struggle. The most obvious example of this principle can be seen when comparing feral and domesticated cats. (Feral cats, by the way, are cats who live outdoors, usually in colonies, and who are not socialized to live with people. Most of them were born feral, but some used to have homes with people before becoming stray and then feral. They may become friendly toward people who give them food, but they generally do not approach people or allow themselves to be petted.) I offer some examples of the differences:

Most domesticated cats forgive easily and readily. Feral cats do not. If a person takes a beloved cat to the vet, the cat will be angry and stressed, but generally not for more than a couple of days. If a person traps a feral cat for trap-neuter-release or vet care purposes, that cat will be extremely wary of the person for months if not years. If a person scolds a house cat or uses a disciplinary spray bottle, the cat will generally forgive the person within 15 minutes. If a person commits the offense of walking too quickly toward an area that is anywhere near a feral cat, that cat will likely hiss at the person during every close encounter for the next many months.

Just as they are slow to forgive a person, feral cats are slow to trust the environment after there has been a threat or disturbance. If an animal or person who seems dangerous enters their territory, they will go into hiding and sometimes not come out for the rest of the day or even for multiple days. Domestic cats will usually wait only a short while after an intruder has been on the premises before popping back out. They seem to trust quickly that the threat has passed.

Male feral cats can be very territorial and fight other cats, even to the death. Domesticated cats can fight, too, but it's less common for them to actually kill each other.

The reflexes of domestic cats are quick, but the reflexes of ferals are wildly faster. Many people report struggling to get their lazy, lovebug, couch-dwelling cats into a cat carrier. Cats have the ability to turn into a furry mass of liquid muscle if they do not want to be held. Now imagine trying to put a feral cat in a carrier. Twice I have made the mistake of thinking that I could pick up a friendly feral cat and put her directly into a cat carrier, and both times I have failed miserably. When I needed to capture my 8-year-old female feral friend, Martha, whom I could easily pet and even put on my lap, I figured I could pet her for a while and then swiftly put her in the carrier before she realized what was happening. Everything was going as planned – I had the carrier open next to me and was petting Martha on my lap and she was purring. I grabbed her and almost had her all the way in the carrier when of course I felt a sharp pain in my hand and then, less than three full seconds later, saw Martha 40 yards away on the neighbor's porch. My mom saw it more clearly than I did and said that Martha's initial spring from my grasp got her about 10 yards away and then she appeared to actually fly the next 30 yards or so. My mom, however, had not seen Martha bite me (and didn't believe me until I showed her the blood dripping from my fingertip), which means that Martha had bitten me, escaped my grasp, leapt in an impressive arc, and gotten far away so quickly that our human eyes could not register each part of the event. I wish I had the whole interaction on video so that I could play it back in slow motion.

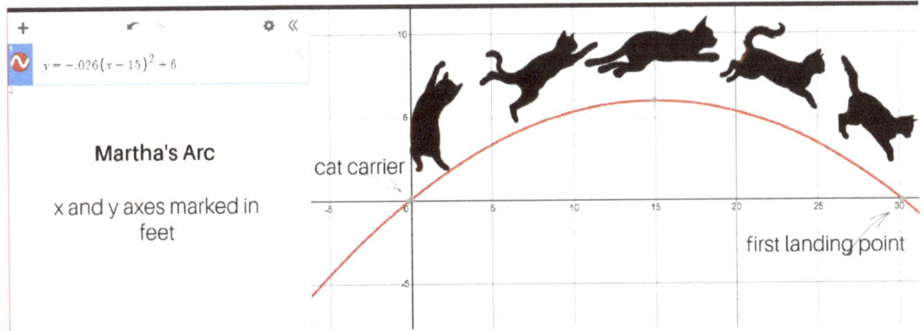

I've taken to assessing cats (and people) using basic binary categories:

hard-working/lazy
giving/taking
introverted/extroverted
curious/bored
questioning/accepting
fighting/fleeing
satisfied/jealous.

This system yields 128 possible combinations. I also like using personality tests such as Myers-Briggs, which has only four binaries, yielding 16 personality types. Knowing one's own type could help a person choose a career path or assist employers in matching workers with the positions for which they are best suited. It could help people understand their reactions and relationships better. I'm not sure that knowing a cat's personality type will have any practical benefits, but I know that many people enjoy any insight they can gain into the lives and inner workings of their feline friends. I have amused myself by taking Myers-Briggs quizzes from the imagined perspective of different cats to determine their personality types. I've included those personality test results in each cat's story in this book.

5

A Feral Cat Colony

When I moved to Alabama in 2018, I slowly got to know the colony of feral cats living around my parents' house. Every time I visited, I saw some of the cats and sometimes helped my mom feed them. Every morning, she carefully prepared their food on six or seven individual paper plates. She would put some canned food in the middle, then a ring of leftover meat, and then an outer ring of Costco rotisserie chicken bits. The first time I helped her, she was clearly dissatisfied with my plate presentation. I learned to take it more seriously, although I remained skeptical about the cats' interest in culinary aesthetics.

When I realized that the colony was growing, I looked into options for getting some of them spayed and neutered. I found out that the local Humane Society ran a trap-neuter-release program (TNR); local residents could bring trapped cats to the shelter (where they would be kept overnight before being transported to a clinic) and then pick them up a couple of days later. In addition to being spayed or neutered, the cats are given rabies vaccinations, and their ears are "tipped." The tip of one ear is cut off flat so that the cats can be easily identified after they are released and not be targeted for TNR again. Over the course of about seven months, I trapped thirteen cats and learned a lot about different feral cat personalities and trapping techniques.

While getting more acquainted with the cats I wanted to trap, I realized that there was a binary personality category that I had not really thought about before: bold/watchful. I found that each cat fell into one of these two categories. Knowing which kind of cat I was dealing with made it easier to catch them.

BOLD. Some feral cats venture boldly into any situation, confident in their ability to fight their way out of it if necessary. These tend to be somewhat less intelligent, or at least less clever about strategizing. They show less capacity for shifting perspectives, and their reactions are easier to anticipate than those of their more introspective and less physically courageous peers. They are the easiest to trap, as they'll generally walk right into the trap to get the food. Of course, once the door slams shut on them, they can become frantic and hurt their noses trying to get out.

WATCHFUL. Some feral cats remain watchful, quietly observing all elements within their environment. They reflect upon the behavior of others and trust no one. To anticipate their behavior, one must understand what predictions they are making and what conclusions they have drawn about others and the environment. They are difficult to trap, as they will immediately be suspicious of the trap. Even if they are tempted by the bait, they will be very hesitant to set a paw inside.

Cassie (watchful), Marty (bold), Princess (watchful)

My very first trapping attempt went well for me because I targeted a bold one. Little Grey was about 9 months old, very adventurous, and quite slender – so slender and lightweight, in fact, that when she marched into the box trap to get the food, she did not spring the door shut behind her. She crouched there eating the tuna with her little paws resting on top of the spring plate. I crept over quickly while she was still eating and I manually sprang the trap door closed. Then I put her in the back seat of my car and drove her to the shelter. I was expecting her to thrash and yowl, but she was silent and cute-looking the whole time. I wanted to reach in and pet her cute little head SO badly, but I resisted the temptation.

When I called the shelter two days later to find out when I could come get her, I learned that she had to be quarantined at the vet clinic for 10 days because she had bitten a vet tech so fiercely that the poor woman had to go to the emergency room. I don't know exactly what happened, but I can imagine that the vet tech looked at cute, silent Little Grey and thought "Oh my gosh, what a CUTE little cat! I will pet her!"

When I picked up Little Grey and brought her back to her home, she readjusted quickly. She instantly knew where she was, went to the food dish, greeted her cat friends, and resumed her normal activities.

My second capture was another bold one. This time it was a male I called Tough Guy. He went right into the trap and the door sprang shut instantly. He thrashed quite a bit but did not yowl. I took him right to the shelter and picked him up two days later. While I was carrying the trap to a wooded spot in his home territory to release him, he somehow managed to force his way out of the trap in mid-air and took off like a shot. Thank goodness that had not happened in my car! Lesson learned: the traps aren't always guaranteed to keep powerful animals contained, so it's best to use zip ties on all edges, making sure to tighten them completely and cut the ends off cleanly so the cat can't chew on them.

I worked my way through the rest of the bold cats, one by one. They were males of various ages who were led by their overconfidence right into my trap. Three of them were only about four or five months old, so I took them directly to the spay/neuter clinic and then I managed to find people to adopt them.

Then I had to start working on the watchful cats. I targeted them individually, but I could not lure any of them into the trap. I baited it and left it zip-tied open so they could go in and out and get used to it, but none of them tried it. I camouflaged it inside and out with leaves. Still no luck. Finally, after a couple of weeks of trying, I concluded that these watchful ones were simply not going to walk into a narrow metallic space, no matter how long it had been in their territory and no matter how good the food in it smelled. They were natural-born skeptics. I couldn't blame them. I like to think that I would be the same way if I were in their position. I've always fallen into the "trust no one" camp myself.

I did some research online and found the Alley Cat Allies website (alleycat.org), which has a lot of helpful information. I then decided to order a Tomahawk drop trap and transfer cage. A drop trap is much larger than a regular box trap and props up so that a cat can walk into and under it and not feel completely enclosed by it. It does not have a mechanism to activate it, though, so a person must be watching and pull the string at the right moment to trap the animal. The person must then be ready to throw a blanket over the trap and hold it down so that the cat cannot escape.

Once my drop trap arrived, I set it up quickly and felt optimistic. I baited it, attached the string, and squatted casually behind a tree, waiting for the targeted cat to come have a look. At least an hour passed. No cat appeared, but a neighbor did show up and ask if I was having trouble with the indoor plumbing.

At last, my targeted cat appeared, sniffed the food, and almost went for it but then noticed me. She glared at me and then left. Time for Plan B. I put the drop trap in the carport near the usual feeding station and then arranged the string around the corner of the house so that I could be completely out of sight. I set up a mirror so that I could watch and know when to pull the string.

Sure enough, the cat appeared, sniffed the food, once again almost went in, but then noticed the mirror and went to investigate. She sniffed it, then saw the string and followed it until she came face-to-face with me. Once again, she glared at me and left. This cat was smart. I gave up for the day.

Okay, time for Plan C. The next day, I parked my car so that I could run the string into it through the window and crouch down out of sight. I baited the trap, got in position, and waited. About 20 minutes later, my target appeared. She sniffed the food from outside the trap and then looked around. She surveyed the area but did not realize I was in the car watching. After about five minutes, she went under the drop trap, I pulled the string, and I got her! I leapt out of the car, grabbed the blanket and threw it onto the top of the trap and then had to put a lot of my weight on it to keep her from escaping. I used my phone to call my mom, who was inside the house, to come bring the transfer cage because I was afraid that if I stepped away, the cat would get out.

This cat thrashed around a bit, but I got her transferred into the cage without too much trouble and took her to the shelter. She glared at me silently during the car ride. I sensed that she was not just confused and scared but also full of regret. She was probably thinking, "I knew it! I knew it! I knew it was a trap! Why did I fall for it?" I felt sorry for her but was glad that she would not be able to have more kittens.

I love kittens, and watching feral kittens grow up is fun, but too many of them die. They are eaten by predators such as coyotes, foxes, and birds of prey. They are killed by dogs and even by territorial male cats. They are run over by cars or killed in engines when people start their cars without realizing there are kittens under the hood. Too many of them die rough deaths too often, and I just don't think cats are in the same category as mice or rabbits. They shouldn't be born to be food for other animals.

When I got my first watchful cat back from the shelter, I kept her in my mom's garage in a cage for the rest of the day and overnight to recover from the spay surgery (the males are usually okay to release as soon as 24 hours after their surgery, but the females need a little more time). She accepted food but glared silently at me. When I opened the garage door and released her, she ran far away but reappeared that evening and quickly readjusted to the routines.

Feeling encouraged by my success, I used the same hiding-in-car system to catch the next watchful one in the drop trap. This cat, whom we called Princess, yowled the whole way to the shelter. She was the first cat who vocalized her distress. Often, feral cats are completely silent around people because they do not wish to communicate with them or have never learned how to. Many cat experts believe that cat vocalizations are primarily intended for communication with people and that cats don't talk much to each other, aside from yowling to issue a threat or defensive warning. Princess, who had never said anything to me before, now had many things on her mind to tell me. When I picked her up from the shelter two days later, the nice lady handed me the cage containing a loudly hissing Princess and the rabies vaccination paper and said, "This is NOT a nice cat!" I laughed and apologized. When I got to the car, I noticed that the paper had some fresh blood on it, and I'm quite sure it wasn't Princess's. I think Princess probably managed to swipe the nice lady through the wire of the cage. During her time in the garage, Princess talked a lot. She did very well when I released her, though, and did not go very far at all.

One by one, I trapped the other cats successfully. The last one was a skinny tortoiseshell cat I called Tortie. She did not want to walk into the trap area, but the smelly tuna finally proved too difficult for her to resist. Interestingly, when I pulled the string and the trap fell, she remained still rather than thrashing around. The poor little thing just quietly surrendered. When I picked her up after her surgery, I learned that she had been in heat, so the clinic staff recommended that I keep her confined for a week instead of just an extra day. I set up a larger cage in my mom's garage and kept Tortie there for the week. She was quiet and let me touch her, but I wasn't sure if she liked being petted so I didn't over-do it. She ate plenty, so she gained a little weight while in captivity. When I released her, she disappeared, and I found out later that a lady way down the street had been feeding her for the past year or two and was wondering where Tortie was for that week in the garage.

In 2020, my parents had to move to a smaller, more manageable house without stairs, so I bought their house and took over the care of the cat colony. The following year, I decided to have some renovations done and put the house on the market. But what about the cats? I couldn't leave them, not knowing if the next occupant of the house would take care of them.

In the almost three years that I had been helping care for the cats, we had lost three to cars and predators, found homes for three, and let one return to her real caretaker down the street. That left six cats that I felt responsible for, so I decided to take them with me when I moved. I bought another house in town with a nice back yard and had a 6-foot chain link fence installed with Purrfect cat-proof fencing on top of it. Still aching from the loss of the three that I had known and loved, I was determined that I would keep these six safe from the dangers of the outside world while allowing them to live their feral lives.

I now faced the daunting task of trapping feral cats that had been trapped before - and I had to get it done before the new owners took possession of the house. I set up the drop trap over the feeding station and left it there for days. The idea was for all of the cats to get used to it and have the experience of eating under it without being trapped. I knew that several of them would not go under it, though, so I put food next to it as well as under it so they would at least have to get used to being near it. I set up a camera so that I could see who actually went under it, and I left food out overnight. Of course, that meant that I was attracting creatures other than cats, which is generally not a good idea. My camera caught a raccoon and possum eating under the trap at the same time. A fox also came, as well as a neighbor's big bully cat. Finally, by the fifth or sixth night, most of my target cats were eating under the trap. I suspect that some of them had watched the others go under the trap, eat, and leave before they were willing to do it themselves.

could've trapped a possum and raccoon

could've trapped a fox

The only cat who would not go under the trap was Princess. I tried using treats to lure her closer and closer to the trap, hoping that she would lose her fear of it. I crouched not far from the trap and gave her a couple of treats, which she ate. Then I tossed a couple more under the trap. She walked toward the trap, saw the treats under it, stopped short, turned and looked at me, and let out a series of loud, complaining yowls. She was very mad indeed. Her behavior confirmed my suspicion that she understood the trap, knew that I was trying to trap her, and was determined not to fall victim to my wily ways.

Over the course of the next couple of weeks, I trapped five cats and transferred them across town to my new yard. I was worried that I might never catch Princess. I stopped putting food anywhere except under the trap, so she was getting hungry. Early one morning, when I was fairly certain she hadn't eaten in about 24 hours, I put some warm, smelly Costco rotisserie chicken under the trap and hid in the car. She showed up and could not resist the chicken. I got her! I quickly drove her to her new home, and I got an earful the whole way there. She had some choice words for me.

Cassie and Princess allow a box turtle to share their food

6

Feral Cats Adjust to New Territory

Feral cats typically become very bonded with each other and with their territory, so moving them can cause major trauma. I would not have done it if I had not had a cat fence in place at the new location. They would have run away immediately in an attempt to find their way back home and would surely have been killed by cars or predators.

After consulting with a local fencing company, I decided to have a six-foot chain link fence installed around my back yard, with the Purrfect Fencing system at the top. The fence builders communicated with Purrfect Fence to ensure proper installation. After the work was completed, I carefully inspected the fence at the top and bottom and tried to look at everything from a cat's-eye view to locate any weak spots in my enclosure system. To be on the safe side, I overestimated the cats' abilities, imagining that they could dig under things and leap higher than they actually could. I thought about the dangers of dogs, rabbits, and other creatures digging into the yard from outside of it, so I ordered dig-defense barriers and pounded them into the ground on the exterior of the fence. I zip-tied extra Purrfect cat-proof material at the bottom of the fence in some places. Then I freaked out about the idea of coyotes jumping over the fence and into the yard. I ordered coyote rollers to put at the top of the fence on some sides. I started to feel less paranoid. I had a cat door installed so that the cats could access the shed. But then I looked around and realized that the yard seemed boring for cats. So I spent half a day planting bushes and forsythia and arranging boxes and bins on the patio. I got the two "Kitty Tube" insulated cat shelters from the other house and put them in two different spots in the yard. I also went online and ordered some wooden cat houses, which would arrive later. Finally, I felt ready to start relocating the cats.

Here's a little discussion of each of the six feral cats, in the order that I brought them to my new home.

Cassie

Cassie has an ISTJ personality type. Introverted, observant, thinking, and judging, she tends to be reserved and logical and generally avoids drama. She can also be stubborn.

Cassie is a female short-haired black cat with a white bib and a bobtail who was born in 2015 and grew up in my parents' back yard with three sisters and a brother.

As a kitten, she spent much of her time under the hood of my parents' car, next to the battery. One morning, my mom opened the hood and Cassie and three other kittens leapt out and scattered in different directions, leaving one little kitten behind. That kitten let my mom pick her up and pet her, so my mom adopted her and named her Bright Eyes. My parents tried to catch the others over the course of the next few weeks but never succeeded. Cassie and her sister, Beauty, came for food every day, but their brother and sister later disappeared. They must have found another territory nearby because they reappeared once every several months.

Cassie and Beauty were about the same age as Princess, who was from another litter in the same territory. They played together as kittens and they all became mothers at about the same time. As is often the case in feral cat colonies, they raised their kittens together, sharing the duties of motherhood. Cassie was not the most patient of mothers and had a rather low tolerance for kitten shenanigans. She appeared to tire more easily than the other moms and often walked away to take a break.

Cassie seemed very content around other cats but was extremely skittish around people. By the time I arrived in 2018, Cassie had become a healthy adult with predictable comings and goings and a definite feral attitude. She loved an older alpha male cat called Marty. Marty was a long-haired tabby and was likely her grandfather but also, I'm afraid, her husband and brother-in-law. Marty was a busy boy. Princess also loved Marty, and she and Cassie took turns spending time with him. Sometimes all three of them would snuggle together peacefully. At other times, Princess would swat Cassie and tell her to leave Marty alone. Sometimes at night they would all sleep in different places, and then in the morning there would be a joyous reunion. Usually, Princess would find Marty first and would prance around him in circles. A few times, I saw Princess run to Marty and literally bounce over him in an expression of sheer delight. Cassie was not quite as expressive but seemed equally pleased to see Marty in the mornings.

Sadly, Marty was one of the three that we lost. For many months in a row, he had been showing up to the feeding area on time twice a day and hanging out in the garden most of the rest of the time. Then one day, a couple of months before I moved out, he simply did not appear for breakfast. I looked for him for days and then weeks and found no trace of him. He was probably about 11 years old, which is old for a feral cat. He was aggressive and territorial, so he may have picked a fight with a younger male who defeated him. He may also have been caught by a predator.

So Cassie was left without her closest companion. She was the first one I trapped to take to the new home, and she seemed utterly defeated once I had her in the transfer cage. I left her on the back patio for a little while so that she could get used to the sights and smells of the new yard. I put food and water where she could see it and smell it so that she would know where it was. I knew she would take off as soon as I opened the cage door, but I figured that once she realized she could not get out of the yard, she would remember where the food was and come back to the patio.

I was fairly sure that my fence system would work, but I was still nervous about letting Cassie out. I took a deep breath, removed the cage door, and stepped back. She blinked a couple of times and then shot out and ran in a straight line to the fence. She took a couple of bounding leaps up it, which would have easily taken her up and over a normal fence, but then she hit the Purrfect cat-proof part and stopped. Confused, she dropped back down. Then she frantically ran at the fence at several other places, with the same result each time.

She soon settled down and chose a spot to sit right next to the fence at the top of a slope, as far away from the patio as she could get. It was already dark, so I went inside, figuring that the less she saw of me, the less stressed she would be. I paced around inside, worried about her, but I finally decided to just go to bed and not go back outside.

Around 2:00 a.m., I was awakened by meowing at my window. "Oh, wow!" I thought. "Cassie wants to talk to me! Maybe she wants in! That's weird." I went outside and saw a black cat with a long tail. Not Cassie. This cat was throwing itself at the fence, unsuccessfully attempting to get out. It was frenzied. The cat landed on Cassie a couple of times after its failed fence-jumping attempts, so she darted into the shed, which I thought was rather smart of her. So, my enclosure system had captured a neighborhood cat and now I had to coax it to the gate so that I could let it out without also letting Cassie out. It took at least 20 minutes for the cat to calm down, behave rationally, and correctly interpret my wild "Go this way!" instructions. Lesson learned: do not leave the garbage can on the outside of the fence close enough for a cat to use it as a launching pad to get inside the fenced yard (unless you want more cats). Cat-proof fences are designed to keep animals IN, not OUT.

For the next three days, Cassie stayed in the shed all day. I stuck food in there through the cat door and she ate it. She would come out at night and prowl around the yard, even braving the patio, which must have seemed dangerously close to where she knew the bad person lived. Then I brought the next feral cat to the yard, which improved her life considerably.

Cassie in her new territory

Sibling

Sibling has an ESTP personality type. Mostly extroverted and always observant, he is quick to notice even the slightest change in his environment. Although cautious around new people, he enjoys prospecting and taking risks.

Sibling, born in late 2016, is a short-haired classic tabby cat ("classic tabby," I recently learned, is the name of a specific type of coat pattern). He had a brother who was super cute. My mom loved the super cute brother and just called this sibling "Sibling" because she was not sure about his gender. Unfortunately, the super cute one disappeared at a young age, leaving Sibling on his own with a sadly generic name. Sibling disappeared for a few months and then reappeared and seemed to want to be friends with Princess. He would make advances, but she swatted him away and hissed at him. She was loyal to Marty and apparently not interested in having another mate. Sibling also tried befriending various others but consistently met with rejection. He typically lingered on the periphery of the social activity, staying near the others only at meal times. I felt a bit sad for him.

A few months before I was ready to trap and relocate the cats, I realized that Sibling regularly spent his nights in the storm drain at the far side of the house. In the mornings, I would take the food to the feeding station and then walk over to the storm drain and yell "Breakfast!" into it and then walk away. Sibling would always give me time to get back inside the house before he popped out. When he arrived at the food station, he behaved selfishly, gobbling up more than his fair share and forcing the other cats to stay away until he had eaten his fill. No wonder the girls did not accept Sibling's offers of companionship. They preferred Marty, who was always a gentleman and let his girlfriends and relatives eat first.

When I first got Sibling to the new yard, it was after dark, so I decided to put some food in his cage and leave him confined all night. I put a sheet over the top but left the front uncovered so that he could see out – and so that Cassie could see him if she made her nightly rounds. A few hours later, I watched Cassie come check out his cage. They sniffed each other through the cage and both seemed unbothered. I'm sure they recognized each other's scent. Cassie appeared comfortable walking around the cage and even sat down not far from it.

The next morning, I let Sibling out. He flew to the fence and tried to get over it but failed. He repeated his attempts everywhere, much more vigorously than Cassie had. I worried that he might succeed. But he didn't. The Purrfect fence worked. My presence agitated him, so I went inside. He paced back and forth in front of the fence for a while and then found the shed and went inside it. Cassie was already in there, so I listened carefully for any signs of fighting. They were quiet, and I didn't see either of them again until dusk. Sibling hopped out of the shed first and prowled around. He found one of the two "Kitty Tube" houses I had set up in the yard and went inside it. I had left the old blankets from the other house inside of them, so it would have smelled familiar to him. When Cassie came out a little while later, she looked more confident. She strolled around the yard, stretched, pawed at insects, and then came to the patio and lounged. It really seemed to me that the presence of Sibling put her a bit more at ease.

Duchess

Duchess has an ISFJ personality type. Extremely introverted and shy, she strongly prefers to keep to herself for most of each day. She is open to friendships but tends to take the role of the supporter and audience member rather than being an interactive participant.

Duchess was born in secret, probably to Beauty, probably in late 2018 or early 2019. She has long black and white fur with a little Charlie Chaplin mustache. She came to eat every night after dark and spent the days in a shed or the neighbor's driveway or carport. Of all of the feral cats, she seemed the most feral, truly frightened of people. While the other cats would keep me company while I did yard work or walked around the garden, Duchess would flee in terror if she saw me step outside. I briefly considered leaving her behind when I moved since she did not like me, but I could not bear to think of her there alone without a reliable food source and with the woodland predators around. She has a pudgy type of body with fairly short legs and no tail, so she is not as fast or as nimble as many cats. She bumbles along fearfully. I figured that she would at least be safe, well-fed, and in the company of familiar cats at the new place.

I trapped Duchess a few days after I caught Sibling, and I took her to the new place fairly early in the morning. I left her on the patio for a couple of hours before opening her cage to release her. She did not run out right away, so I left her alone and went inside. After venturing out, she ran to the fence and made two sadly feeble attempts to get out. When she realized she could not get over the fence, she walked the perimeter of the whole yard one and a half times, noticed the cat door to the shed, and went inside. Once again, I listened for trouble because I knew that Cassie and Sibling were in the shed at the time. There was no problem, though. I left them alone and used the cat door to put food inside the shed in the afternoon. I did not want to open the door and alarm them all. That night, they came out one by one – first Sibling, then Cassie about 30 minutes later, and finally Duchess about an hour after that. Duchess stayed low to the ground and close to the fence and patrolled the perimeter for a couple of hours before returning to the shed.

Duchess

Martha

Martha has an ENFP personality type. She is quite extroverted and makes friends readily. She seeks joy and does not want to interfere with anyone else's happiness. Good-natured, curious, and optimistic, she is generally pleasant to be around. She avoids conflict and forgives quickly.

Martha is by far the oldest of the six feral cats that I took to the new place, probably born in 2012. She is a long-haired gray tabby with a bobtail and a big mane. When I first met Martha, I declared that she was hardly feral at all. She meowed at me and let me pet her! As I found when I tried to pick her up and put her in a cat carrier, though (as described in an earlier section), I realized that she actually does have more of the traits of a feral cat than of a housecat. She also has a cute habit of bouncing laterally if she is startled. The other feral cats seem to run quickly if spooked, but Martha does a single long-arced sideways bounce before running away.

Since she allowed herself to be petted, I thought I might convince her to become an indoor cat. I tried coaxing her inside little by little over the course of a few weeks and finally convinced her to come into the laundry room when it was freezing outside; as soon as I closed the door, she yowled most pitiably and jumped at the door, desperate to get out. She would rather endure a night of high winds and temperatures in the 20's than be in a warm place inside a house.

When I got Martha to the new yard, dusk was falling, so I decided to let her out of the cage soon after setting her down. I knew that Sibling would be along soon and she would recognize him. Just like the other three before her, she ran to the fence immediately after exiting the cage and tried to climb it. She made attempts in three places and then seemed to understand that she would not be able to escape. She looked around, confused, and I called to her. I was hoping she would behave like she always did and come over and let me pet her and reassure her, but of course she was too stressed. I worried that the relocation might permanently alter her demeanor and personality. I went inside and watched through the window and on camera.

Soon, as predicted, Sibling emerged from the shed, and he spotted Martha right away. He walked over to her casually and they touched noses. She was clearly in a stressed state, but he seemed fairly relaxed. He had been in the yard for about a week at this point. Martha ran from place to place in the yard – to the fence, to a bush, back to the fence, to the patio, and so on. She couldn't settle down anywhere. I waited a couple of hours and then went back outside to try to talk to her. No luck, so I just left food and went back inside.

A loud thunderstorm woke me up in the wee hours. I felt so bad for Martha out there in the storm in a strange yard. I looked at the camera footage and could see that Cassie, Sibling, and Duchess had all gone into the shed at least an hour before the rain had started. I could see Martha pacing around, though. She came to the patio for cover but, surprisingly, did not stay. The patio must have seemed too much like an unknown human dwelling and she didn't trust it. Instead, she huddled next to the fence, getting wet. I couldn't think of anything to do, so I went back to sleep for a couple of hours.

Martha

At first light, I went outside with a towel. The rain had stopped, and Martha was sitting by the fence, soaking wet and stressed. I called her softly but she remained frozen in place. I walked toward her and she ran a few yards away. I tried coaxing for about five minutes. Then I switched from a sweet, calming voice to a firm tone. "Martha! Stop this nonsense right now! We are friends! You will come here right now and I will dry you off!" She meowed. "I mean it!" I continued. "You come here right now!" She meowed again and, surprisingly, took a few steps toward me. I crouched down very low and waddled slowly to her. Then I sat down on the wet grass, put the towel on my lap, and called her again, using an in-between-sweet-and-firm tone of voice. She moved a little closer, and I petted her head and she came all the way over to me. I quickly got her on my lap and toweled her off. She slowly turned back into the sweet Martha that I was used to. I cuddled her for a little while and then tried to explain where she was and why I had brought her there. I showed her the Kitty Tubes, the shed, and the patio. I went back inside and she dove into a Kitty Tube.

She stayed in the tube for the rest of the morning and afternoon, but she came out when I called her for dinner. That night, she and Sibling met up and prowled around the perimeter for a while. I watched them as they sat side by side looking through the fence.

I was relieved to see Martha adjust quickly to her new life. The next morning, she came right over to me and behaved as she had in her old territory. She let me pet her and trotted around confidently.

Beauty

Beauty has an ISTJ personality type. Like her sister Cassie, she is introverted, observant, thinking, and judging, but she is even more solitary and watchful. She is a strategic thinker, slow to take social or physical risks.

Beauty is a long-haired black female with a splendid mane and a bobtail. My mom watched her grow up and noticed that she was the most likely to keep to herself. She did not fight with the others, but she preferred her own company to theirs. She would watch them from a distance and, even if she showed up first to the feeding area, would wait for everyone else to come and eat before she ventured to the food. She would pick a spot where she would spend most of her time during daylight hours every day for about six months, and then she would pick a new spot. She typically stayed in or under the shed at night. She never said a word, but she trusted my mom and would go to her when called. It took me a long time to gain her trust, and on one exciting day, I finally got a good slow blink from her.

When I got Beauty to the new yard, I left her in the cage for about a half an hour before releasing her into the night. She was not frantic, but she did try to climb the fence. Cassie, Sibling, and Martha watched her one and only attempt, after which she turned and looked at them. I could sense the silent communication.

Sibling: "There's no point."

Beauty: "There's no way out, is there? That's why you're all still here."

Cassie: "Exactly."

Martha (bouncing a little): "But it's okay, we're happy."

Beauty did not try to climb the fence again. She looked dejected and just sat by the fence for hours. Later, I saw on the camera that she found one of the Kitty Tubes and went in. The next morning, I brought her breakfast on a plate and set it outside the tube. She waited for me to back away and then she came partially out like a turtle and ate.

Beauty

Princess

Princess has an ISTP personality type. She is more introverted than extroverted, but not nearly as introverted as Cassie, Beauty, and Duchess. She does enjoy having others take an interest in her and is even open to letting them into her personal space on a case-by-case basis. She tends to act in an unpredictable manner, being friendly to people or cats for a period of time and then attacking them for no particular reason at another time.

Princess is a short-haired tabby with a bobtail. She is the smallest of the group but certainly the toughest of the females. She was a nurturing mother and babysitter who knew how to raise a kitten with a firm paw while still showing lots of love. Cassie and Beauty would take off for the day and Princess would sit in the middle of all of the frolicking kittens and let them play.

Princess is smart, and she seems to enjoy tempting humans to pet her and then denying them. When approached by a person she knows (me or my mom), she will make eye contact and then rub up against a nearby object in a friendly way. She has even acted like she was going to rub against my legs but then stopped and rubbed against a tree or post instead. Every time I have reached a hand out to pet her, she has approached it as if she were thinking of allowing contact and then swiped it, usually drawing blood. I imagine Princess grandly saying, "You may admire the Princess, you may speak to the Princess, you may give the Princess treats, but you must not touch the Princess."

When I finally caught her and brought her to the new yard, she was inconsolable. We arrived in the morning and she was yowling in the cage, so I let her out right away. She ran to the fence and tried twice to get over it, with no luck. Unlike the others, she then immediately went to work trying to get under or through the fence. I saw her stick her head through the chain link and I started to panic. (I had always heard that cats can get through any space that they can get their head through, but I now realize that this is not always true.) I started rushing around, reinforcing the bottom of the fence with bricks, Purrfect fence material, and random objects from the patio. I chased her away from the fence. She settled down under a bush and cried. I felt terrible seeing her so miserable. I got some treats and went to talk to her. I crouched down and we made eye contact. She begged me to take her back home to her territory. I explained the situation but she did not understand. She did eat the treats, though, so I took that as a good sign.

Cassie, Sibling, and Martha heard all the commotion and came to investigate. They each greeted Princess and touched noses, obviously all recognizing each other. Princess was still upset and meowed questions at them. She paced around the bushes and then saw Beauty sitting right in front of the fence. She ran up to her and tried to get through the fence next to her. When she failed, she buried her nose in Beauty's fur for a few moments, reassuring herself with the familiar scent. Beauty sat there unmoved, offering neither comfort nor discouragement. I sat next to Princess for a while and then left her alone so that I could work some more on reinforcing the bottom of the fence.

Princess remained stressed and upset for three full days and nights, but then she started to settle down. Unlike Martha, who had suddenly felt afraid of me on the first day of the move, Princess never felt scared of me and, if anything, recognized me as the only one who might be able to help her. She continued to allow me to approach her, talk to her, and give her food and treats. She never stopped eating, as many stressed-out feral cats do. In the end, she accepted the new territory and even seemed to like it.

Princess frowning

7

Cat Relationships

About two weeks after the six-cat colony was settled into the new territory, Sibling fell in love with Martha. He had been enjoying his walks with her every night and morning and was pleased by the feeling of friendship, but then something changed for him. He wanted more than friendship. He was ridiculously googly-eyed and in love. He watched her, he followed her, he took every opportunity to rub against her, cuddle with her, and sleep next to her.

Martha accepted his advances but felt a bit overwhelmed by them. She would have been happy to maintain the friend-level relationship. She had always been peaceful around other cats, but never clingy. If they wanted to be friends, she would be friendly in a fairly casual way. If they wanted to pick a fight, she would just walk away.

Princess noticed right away when Sibling and Martha became a couple. This observation led her to reconsider her longstanding dismissal of Sibling. "Perhaps he should be mine after all," Princess thought. "He is the only male, and my Marty is gone. A couple of years ago, Sibling used to pester me to be his girlfriend. Well, perhaps now is the time." Princess decided to get his attention. Every time she saw him, which was often, she would slap him, then lick his head, and then offer her own head to be licked. If he didn't immediately reciprocate, she would slap him until he got the right idea. He seemed intimidated. He would get a scared look on his face and then hesitantly give her a few licks on the forehead. Then he would make his excuses and go look for Martha every time.

The love triangle went on like this for weeks. Sibling really only had eyes for Martha, but he would give some attention to Princess to avoid provoking one of her outbursts of aggression. Fortunately, Princess was content to sleep in her own cat house, leaving Sibling free to go curl up with Martha wherever she was.

Then one day, Cassie decided that if Princess was getting attention from Sibling, then she should do the same. After all, they had shared Marty. Now that Marty was gone, they would have to share the next best thing: Sibling. Cassie approached Sibling one morning after he had finished his perimeter walk with Martha. Cassie offered him a cordial head bump and then requested that he accompany her on a perimeter walk of their own. Since Martha did not mind at all and, in fact, seemed only too pleased to get a break from him, Sibling led Cassie to the fence and began escorting her along the pavers. They stopped here and there to sniff the grass and touch noses, and at the end of their little venture, Sibling allowed Cassie to walk around him in circles, brushing her entire side against him. Content, she slowly walked away and found a cat house to perch in.

Sibling pranced proudly back to the patio to find Martha. He felt that Cassie's display of affection would make him even more appealing now. "Hey Martha!" he called. "Do you see how attractive I am? Everyone wants to be with me. You should consider yourself lucky that I have chosen you."

Martha was neither impressed nor unimpressed. She knew that Sibling loved her the most, and she was not jealous of Princess or Cassie.

Each morning thereafter became predictable. Sibling and Martha would get up, walk to the food dish together, eat, and then go on a walk around the yard. While they walked, Cassie and Princess ate. Then Cassie would join Sibling on a walk and give him some good head and side rubs. When he returned to the patio, Princess would slap him around a little and make him groom her before letting him go see his beloved Martha again.

What about Beauty? She had always been a solitary observer of the other members of her colony. But about six months after Cassie befriended Sibling, Beauty, too, decided that she might have some feelings for the boy. He had been polite to her and had tried to touch noses with her a few times, but she had always rebuffed him. She did not like physical contact. Now, though, she thought she might like to try having a companion. She approached him one morning after he had finished his walks with Martha and Cassie. "I think you asked me last week if I wanted to be friends," she said to him. "At the time, I said no. I have changed my mind. I want to be your friend." He understood. He head-butted her in response. She immediately banged her head into his cheek. He walked toward the fence and she followed. Instead of leading her on a walk, though, he plunked down in the grass and looked at her. She rubbed against his side and then head-banged his cheek again. He looked pleased. Then she sat down next to him so that their sides were touching. They remained together for about an hour. In the days that followed, Beauty developed this new routine of sitting with him for about an hour, mid-morning.

Sibling had spent years in the old territory longing for companionship and facing only rejection. Now he had four girlfriends, and his chest was nearly bursting with pride. He was altogether a new cat.

Sadly, just as human relationships can fail, cat love doesn't always last forever. Beauty and Sibling broke up after just four months of dating. Neither one seems to know why. They avoid each other now and have awkward exchanges on the patio.

Sibling gets love from Beauty (3 photos) and snuggles with Cassie

Top left: Sibling snoozes with his beloved Martha; Top right: Sibling displays happy tail, surrounded by his new admirers; Bottom, left to right: Sibling, Princess, Beauty, Cassie

Cats Can Also Fall in Love with People

Anyone who has ever taken a liking to a cat who was standoffish at first but then became loving and affectionate knows what a nice feeling it is to win the love of a cat. I'll just highlight a couple of examples.

Shortly after moving into a shared house (decades ago), I started trying to make friends with the resident black cat, Cattywampus. She was friendly to everyone in general but did not seem to have any favorites. I observed her habits and offered affection only when she seemed to want it. I began an evening routine of sitting and reading near her after dinner. One night, after about a week of following this routine, I noticed that she seemed interested in cozying up to me. I petted her for a long time. The next evening, she looked for me to repeat the previous night's activities. The following morning, I opened my bedroom door and she was waiting for me. That was it – she loved me.

Years later, I was living in a condo with my own cat when a neighbor downstairs moved in with an indoor/outdoor adult male cat. He greeted me every time I got out of my car, so I would pet him. Then he would follow me up the stairs and swat me on the leg if I stopped petting him too soon. This routine went on for weeks and he became increasingly playful. Then one day, while I was driving slowly toward my parking spot, I saw him come around the corner of the building, notice my car, and then dash back behind the wall. After I got out of my car and started walking toward the building, he sprang out in an attempt to surprise me and then gleefully rubbed up against my legs. I really felt like he was laughing at his trick. After that, he tried to surprise me every day. It was super cute.

8

A One-Act Play

Cast:
Boss, male
Executive Assistant, female
4 young women - Princess, Beauty, Duchess, Martha
1 young man - Big Guy

Setting: Large boardroom with side table

Boss is in boardroom setting up computer, papers, books, talking to Executive Assistant who is setting up water on the side table

Boss: I'm not sure how this meeting is going to go. This is the most unusual group of employees I've ever been assigned. At least they all know each other, so I'm assuming they'll work together well.

Assistant: A couple of them were in my office yesterday and I thought they were a bit odd, too. Who hired them?

Boss: I have no idea where they came from. My boss didn't give me any back story on any of them.

Assistant: Hmmm. Interesting. Well, good luck with the meeting! *exits the room*

Five employees enter slowly, looking around, then go to the corners of the room and look around some more. The young man goes over to one of the young women, who quickly hits him twice on the cheek, then backs off. He goes over to another young woman, who rubs her shoulder against his shoulder. During these actions, they are talking a little bit, saying things like Hey! How's it going? Could you back up a little? etc.

Boss: *looking bewildered* Okay everyone, let's all please take our seats so we can get started. Thanks. I haven't had a chance to get to know any of you yet, so let's go around the room and introduce ourselves. *gestures to first young woman* Go ahead.

Princess: *stares quietly, long pause* I'm Princess.

Boss: Okay, good morning, Princess. What is your job?

Princess: I used to take care of the little ones, but they've grown up and moved away. Now I plan strategic exits.

Boss: Hmmm. Okay. And you? *gestures toward male*

Big Guy: Well, I'm Big Guy. I'm in charge of threat assessment and strategic defense systems.

Boss: Okay, awesome. Have there been a lot of threats?

Big Guy: Oh yes! Every day.

Boss: Okay, good to have you then. Next?

Duchess: I'm Duchess. I deal with strategic acquisitions.

Boss: Great! And you?

Beauty: I help with acquisitions but mostly I work in strategic design.

Boss: Sounds amazing! And you?

Martha: I'm in charge of strategic negotiations with outsiders.

Boss: Outsiders? Well, okay, super. I notice you all include the word "strategic" in your job description. So let's start with that today. We need to come up with a strategy to address the emerging competition in our field. As you know, we're already losing ground and could be in serious trouble if we don't act quickly. Any thoughts?

Beauty: Isolate ourselves immediately. Containment is the only way to go.

Big Guy: Attack it. Knock out the competition. Show me where they are and I'll take them down.

Princess: Watch them carefully for weakness and then take advantage of any opening you see to get around them.

Duchess: I'm with Beauty on this one. Hide. I mean, check to see that our position is isolated, enclosed, and not too obvious.

Martha: Observe them carefully, as Princess said, but be prepared to make a friendly gesture and then wait to see what happens.

Boss: *slowly, confused* Okay, I'm not sure what any of you mean. I'm thinking that we need to discuss our efficiency of production as well as marketing strategies here.

Suddenly, Boss accidentally drops a book which lands loudly on the floor. All five employees leap up. Martha then bounds sideways, while Beauty and Duchess duck under the table. Princess and Big Guy run into each other as they both flee to the corner of the room.

Boss: Guys, take it easy. It was just a book dropping. Everything is okay. Could you please come back to your seats?

Employees return to their seats, looking a bit humbled.

Big Guy: We may have overreacted on that one.

Princess: Agreed.

Beauty: You can never be too careful. You remember what happened when

Duchess: Shh! We don't need to talk about that.

Boss: So I was saying that I want to address the threat of competition by looking at both production and marketing.

Assistant walks into the room with a plate of cookies. Employees freak out. Big Guy rushes at her and makes a hissing sound while the other four retreat quickly to the corners and stare at her.

Big Guy: You're a demon straight from the depths of the underworld!

Princess: Like Grendel rising from the deep to attack us!

Beauty: Get away!

Duchess: She's going to kill us for sure this time.

Martha: She might not. Just watch and wait for a minute.

Assistant: Folks, I'm just bringing you some treats. I'll set them down here on the table and leave. Don't you remember I met some of you yesterday?

Big Guy: Okay, slowly, please. Set the treats down ***slowly*** and then back yourself right out that door.

Princess: The treats must be given but then you must leave immediately.

Big Guy approaches the cookies as soon as the assistant has left. Princess swats his arm twice. He backs off and she gets a cookie first. Then Big Guy takes seven cookies, counting them carefully. Martha tries to appear casual as she gets two cookies for herself. Beauty and Duchess watch everyone else intently and wait for them to return to their seats before slowly slinking to the cookie tray to get one each.

Boss: I have to say, I've never seen anyone react like this to my assistant or her cookies. I really feel like you all owe her an apology.

All employees stare blankly at the Boss for a solid minute. Then Princess turns and stares at Big Guy, then slaps him. Then he says Why did you do that? *and she says* No reason.

Boss: So, getting back to business, I want to show you a PowerPoint with some ideas.

Boss turns on laptop, starts PowerPoint, turns it to show them, and loud generic-sounding music signifies the beginning of the slideshow; at the first sound, the employees all look startled and push themselves backward in their chairs and then keep scooting backward and sideways until they are all grouped together at the end of the table, as far as possible from the computer.

Boss: Relax, please! Can you all see the slides from there? Let's just start with the first one. We need to discuss our productivity. What do you think about my proposal for 9-hour shifts with a 1-hour lunch break, five days per week, instead of 10-hour shifts four days per week. Ideas?

Princess: Don't you mean a 1-hour shift with 9 hours of breaks?

Big Guy: Obviously, that's what he means. The other way around makes no sense.

Martha: It's a funny idea, though! Imagine! Work for nine hours, rest for one!

Boss: I'm confused. Are you joking? I need some serious feedback here. Should we move to a 5-day workweek? Would that help our productivity?

Big Guy: A week has seven days. We all have to work all seven days.

Boss: Interesting! So you think we should go to a 7- day work week with, what, 6 - hour shifts?

Princess: A day has 24 hours in it, from sunrise to sunrise.

Boss: You're right! But what's your point?

Princess: I don't have a point. You just seem confused about the number of hours in a day.

Boss: Okay, let's start over. What is the ideal number of hours in a shift that will allow an employee to be the most productive? Too many hours and the employee rate of production slows down too much. Not enough hours and we don't produce enough.

Martha: I can help with this because I have the most experience. Almost 12 years now. Working really hard for half an hour requires about 8 hours of rest. Personally, I find that I'm most productive in spurts of 10 to 15 minutes. But if I have a more challenging project ahead of me, I might spend the full 30 minutes on it.

Big Guy: I'm the same! Martha, sometimes when we work together on a challenge, it cuts down on the time that we each spend. For instance, last week when we caught that

Martha: I don't think you need to mention specifics here.

Big Guy: Oh, okay. Last week when we . . . worked together, we finished off a job in about 15 minutes. It might have taken me the full 30 minutes alone. Then we enjoyed the fruits of our labor together and rested for the next 7 or 8 hours, didn't we?

Martha: Yes, I think that's about right.

Princess: The obvious problem is that you have to be rested when a challenge presents itself. And you never know when that challenge will occur. So, you have to make sure you rest as much as possible when you have the opportunity.

Beauty: I don't understand what you mean by "work" and "productivity."

Duchess: I was about to say the same thing, Beauty. Do watching, thinking, training, and strategizing count as "work"?

Boss: Well, I suppose that's a good question. When I use the term "productivity," I'm specifically referring to the output of the people who work in the factory here manufacturing our product.

Princess: What about all of the people who sit at desks in offices?

Boss: They need to get their work done, too, but we'll leave them out of the discussion about productivity for now.

Princess: Well, then, you can make the factory workers come here whatever hours you want to, but you need to make more places for them to nap. I'm picturing soft surfaces in warm places or in front of windows, with some options in corners or under other objects for an increased sense of safety. Then they'll be as productive as possible during their 30 minutes of work. I think that you'll really see a spike in their speed if they have better-quality rest.

Big Guy, Duchess, Beauty, Martha: Agreed.

Boss: *looking exasperated* All right, well, I'll take that into consideration. Any other ideas?

Duchess: Better-quality rest means absolutely no loud noises. Nobody can rest if there are loud noises.

Boss: *sarcastically* Well, now that we've decided on the new schedule and environment for our factory workers, let's discuss our own work expectations.

Beauty: The chair in my office is too low. I would like a higher one. I think better when I sit up high.

Boss: How high does your chair need to be? Do you mean like a bar stool?

Beauty: Ideally, about 9 or 10 feet off the ground.

long pause

Boss: Okay, I'll see what I can do.

Princess: There are no insects in my office at all.

Boss: Glad to hear it! We pride ourselves on our clean facilities!

Princess: But I think much better when I can have snacks. Do you think if I open my window this summer the cicadas will come in?

Boss: I very much doubt that you'll still be here this summer.

Duchess: Someone came into my office yesterday and took away the balled-up paper that was in the metal container on the floor. I wasn't done with that paper yet. I wanted to tell her to stop, but I felt too scared to say anything.

Martha: That happened to me yesterday, too! That thief should be fired.

Big Guy: I just thought of something. Martha and I could share an office. I could protect her.

Boss: Uh, okay, I'll let the HR department know. Now let's look at the next slide about marketing. This is where we can all work together to have an impact.

Princess: What's the product we want to sell?

Boss: Lawn mowers.

All five employees spring straight upward out of their chairs and frantically run in different directions, bumping into each other several times before all ending up in the same corner of the room.

Duchess: Please sir, don't sell them!

Big Guy: You don't need advertisements. You need public service announcements! And our message to the public is clear: Do not buy these from us OR from the competition!

Boss: *firmly* Okay. I feel like this company is not a good fit for any of you. Do you understand what I'm saying?

All employees suddenly turn back into the cats that they were all along, leaving their human clothes scattered on the floor. They remain in the corner and look at the boss, blinking silently.

***Boss** goes to the door and calls his assistant into the room.*

Boss: *gesturing toward the cats* Take a look at this.

Assistant: Ohhhhhh they were actually cats! Well, that makes a lot more sense now!

Boss: Doesn't it?

The End

9

Core Beliefs of Feral Cats

The best predictor of future behavior is past behavior

Perhaps you've heard the saying that "the best predictor of future behavior is past behavior." We all know that this is generally true, even though we often want to believe that it's not. We make clowns of ourselves trusting that people have changed, or that they will change soon, or that they can behave in a way that they have never behaved before, or that they can suddenly surprise everyone and manifest new drives, motivations, and desires in their lives. Hey, just because she's been divorced or widowed five times doesn't mean you shouldn't marry her. Hey, just because the guy killed his first wife doesn't mean that the suspicious death of his second wife was also a murder. Well, just because a man brutally attacked and killed a stranger for no reason doesn't mean he will do it again if we let him out of prison one day. We have too many people in prison already, right? And everyone deserves a second chance.

Feral cats are much wiser. They would never fall for such a ridiculous line of thinking. They haven't just heard this saying about how to predict behavior – they believe it in the core of their being. I suppose most wild creatures follow this rule as well. They observe the behavior of the other creatures in their environment and make predictions about how those creatures will act and react in all situations. I imagine that if they encounter a creature they've never seen before, they will quickly categorize it based on the characteristics it shares with other known creatures and then predict its behavior accordingly. Eyes in the front of its face, staring at me? Danger! Large with two legs? Danger!

Unfortunately, this core belief of the feral cats has worked against me as I have tried to establish trust. I trapped them and took them to a new place against their will, so they all predict that I will do something similar again. Cassie and Duchess are the most suspicious of me. I look at them and I know what they're thinking: "You can't fool us. We know now what you are. We won't let you get us again. If you try, YOU will be the fool."

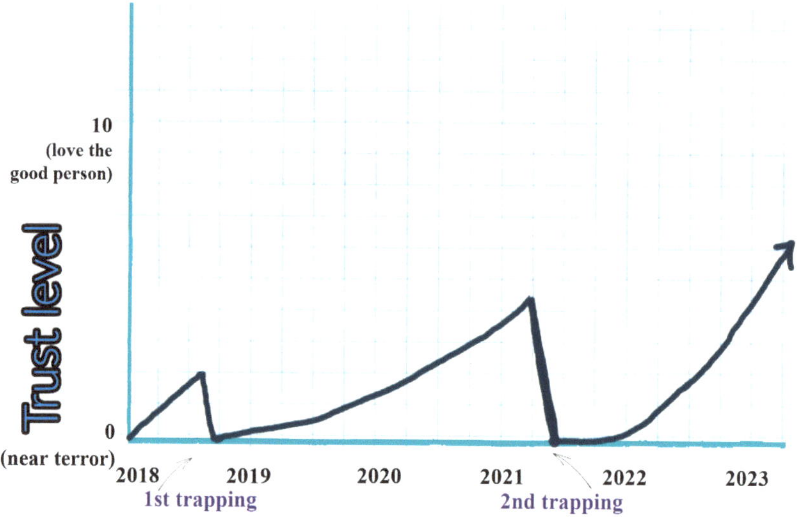

This principle can sometimes work in my favor, though – but very slowly over a long period of time. Example: the lawn mower. When I first mowed their lawn using my relatively small electric lawn mower, I knew they would freak out, and they did. In their original territory, they often had to tolerate loud yard-work machinery, as chainsaws, lawn mowers, and power blowers were used on a fairly regular basis in the neighborhood – but there was no fence preventing them from running far away from the noise. Now, I was using a noisy machine in their space and they could only run to the opposite side of the yard. I worked as quickly as I could, but I know it still traumatized them the first several times I did it. Slowly, though, they came to accept it. They were using their mantra: the best predictor of future behavior is past behavior. If I had not used the mower to hurt them the first ten times I brought it out, perhaps there was actually a reason unrelated to cat-murder that could explain why I was using the offensive machine. By the end of the first summer, they were not made frantic by my mowing. By the end of the second summer, the mower would make them unhappy but not miserable. Now that I'm into our third summer here, I'm noticing that they are starting to be almost (not quite) nonchalant about it. During my most recent mowing session, Princess walked fairly close to me, Martha lounged in the middle of the patio, and Beauty assumed a spot on top of a cat house to observe my work. I've calculated that, if their level of terror began at a 10 (which is the maximum), then there's a half-life of about four years, meaning that they should make it down below a level 2 within their lifetimes.

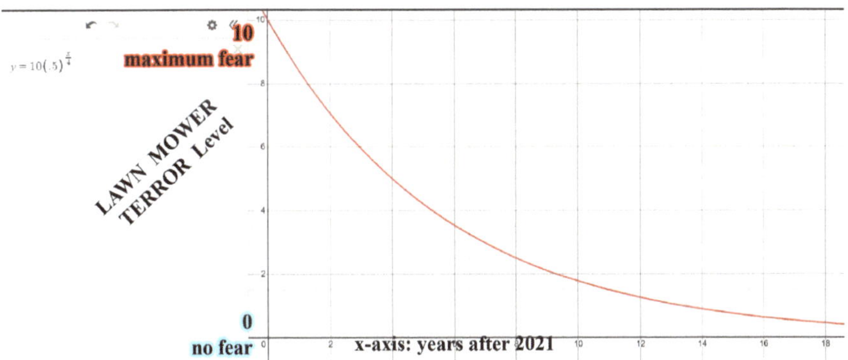

Optimism is not only foolish but dangerous

Consider Mark Twain's quote: "When a man is a pessimist before 48, he knows too much; if he is an optimist after it, he knows too little."

Cats mature much more quickly than slow-growing humans, so if we replace the word "man" with the word "cat," then we need to change the age of 48 to the age of 6 months. Kittens are optimists. They may stumble into the path of another animal and optimistically assume that it is friendly when it may, in fact, be quite dangerous. Adult feral cats are not optimistic, and many domesticated cats are not. I don't think we need to call them pessimists, though. They are, quite simply, realists. They harbor no delusions about life, and they act according to how the environment works for them, not according to how they wish it would work.

There is great significance to the passage of time

Feral cats understand the seasons and the weather, of course. They tend to fatten themselves up in the fall and start losing the weight in the spring. I have found that I have to decrease the quantity of food starting around May or it will just go to waste and attract insects. Then I increase the amount again in late September. Last year, after a solid week of hot days, Princess appointed herself to the role of enforcer at the food dish. When anyone tried to eat the normal amount, she slapped them. "Look at us!" she seemed to be saying. "We're fat! We need to lose this winter weight immediately or we're all going to be miserable. So eat just a little and then get away from the food dish!"

Patience must be boundless

A feral cat knows how to be patient. A mother cat will often leave her kittens in a hiding place and instruct them to stay there while she is gone. Kittens will stay under a car hood, shed, or wood pile doing absolutely nothing and keeping quiet for hours on end. As adults, they will wait patiently in hiding until they are confident that a danger has passed. They will also wait patiently at meal times if a person has established a habit of providing food.

Cassie and Sibling stick their heads out of the cat door of the shed hours after a stranger has been in the yard. They will wait until they are sure the coast is clear.

Routines are important

Like elderly people, feral cats depend on routines and tend not to like surprises. Perhaps because they sense that they are in a vulnerable position, they rely on consistency and routine to minimize their stress and maintain some control over their lives. Also, cats can tell time. If you feed them at the same time two or three days in a row, they will remember that exact time and appear at the feeding station promptly.

Domesticated cats also seem to value routines, by the way. Everybody likes some order in their lives.

Everybody likes to have choices

Just because they like routines doesn't mean they don't like to have choices, though. Feral cats, just like domesticated cats and people, like to have options and the freedom to choose. I have provided 5 cat houses plus the two Kitty Tubes and other soft cat beds and cardboard boxes so that they have plenty of choices. They have formed their own habits and favorite activities. Beauty chooses a new spot every six months or so, Cassie chooses to walk around with Sibling, Sibling chooses to follow Martha around the yard, Martha chooses to follow me around the yard, Duchess chooses to stay in the shed for many daylight hours and to spend more time outside in the dark, and Princess chooses to guard the patio and snack on cicadas in the yard. They all appreciate choices at mealtime, too. Some prefer seafood, some choose poultry, some like dry food the best, and some love wet food.

This core belief applies equally to domesticated cats and human children. I have often found that I get better behavior and compliance from my indoor cats and human students when I give them choices. I want them to do things because they have made the choice themselves, not because I have insisted that they do or don't do something. I might limit their choices to two or three options, but still . . . they have a choice.

Celebrate meal times

When Princess and Sibling see me coming with the food, they rub up against each other in a celebratory display of affection. Beauty also perks up, arches her back a little, and struts around the patio. I have noticed that my little indoor Claude reacts the same way to meal times - especially dinner. He arches and then headbutts Chloe or Cleopatra in a loving way right before I put food in his dish. It is good to celebrate dinner.

There are different ways of being social

Being social can involve walking around together, headbutting, rubbing against each other, sleeping next to each other, sleeping curled up together, or just sitting near each other. Occupying the same space peacefully meets some cats' (and people's) definition of being social. Everyone's different.

Gender roles exist

In many ways just like lions, male ferals defend the territory and impregnate the females. They don't tend to participate in childcare but they do patrol the boundaries and watch over the females. Marty always watched the feeding area and let the girls eat first, especially when they were nursing. He was a classic gentleman. Not Sibling, though. Sibling is more like the lions I've seen on the Discovery channel. He asserts his rights as the male and eats first, not caring if he leaves any for the others. To take a charitable view of his boorish behavior, I might say that he puts his needs first so that he will have the strength to defend the girls if necessary. I must also say, however, that when danger actually presents itself in the form of a maintenance man in the back yard, Sibling typically just runs and hides in the shed without showing much concern for defending anyone. After the danger is over, though, he does offer comfort to Martha and Cassie, giving them rubs and headbutts if they are still seeming skittish.

Most of the female ferals seem to want to attach themselves to a male protector. After their loss of Marty, Princess and Cassie both turned to Sibling and decided that they liked him. The girls shared childcare duties, and they've always seemed happy to hang out together, but they don't snuggle up with each other. They want to snuggle up with the male. I'm not saying same-gender snuggling doesn't happen among cats – it does! My mixed-gender indoor cats will sleep in a catpile on the couch. I'm merely making an observation about the feral cats' impulses toward gender-based bonding within the colony when they perceive themselves to be in an environment that contains threats (and the outdoor world always contains threats).

10

The Indoor Cats' Stories (with Some Tips)

Having six indoor cats (and six outdoor ones) may seem excessive to some people, but I don't find myself at all overwhelmed by them. Each cat's personality creates a unique presence. I imagine that it's similar to having a house full of children. If somebody is missing, the absence is noticed. If one of my cats is gone for the day to the vet, the house feels weirdly empty. Going out of town, even for a day, is difficult with so many cats to tend to, but who needs a vacation when staying home is so fun?

Living with cats requires compromise on both sides. Domestic cats have to give up some of their wildness, accustom themselves to regular communication with people, respect their person's preferred activities, and behave just a little bit more like people than they would probably like to. In return, they get food, water, heating and cooling, protection, regular physical contact and companionship, and, hopefully, some amusement. People have to learn how to communicate effectively in cat language, get to know their cats' personalities and preferred activities, act a little bit more cat-like, and give up a portion of their income, time, and furniture to meet the cats' needs. In return, they get companionship, loads of entertainment, and new insights into the meaning of life on Earth.

Allow me to present the story of each indoor cat individually, with some related tips on cat care at the end of each one.

* * *

Claude

Claude has an ESFP-T personality type, sometimes called "The Entertainer." He is social and adventurous but can become bored easily. He cannot tolerate being alone and must have a person or cat in his presence at all times. If left alone, he cries unceasingly.

Sept. 5, 2021

Claude was just four months old and still trying to get used to his cat body. He found it uncomfortable and weird. He sought reassurance from other creatures. Was everything okay? Was he on the right planet? Was he supposed to be someone or something else? He vocalized these questions continually, never satisfied with anyone's answers.

Claude had spent the last many days in a wire cage in a loud room with other cats. Now the cage door was open and he could see a new room with a soft floor. There was an unfamiliar person and two other cats whom he recognized as having been in the cages next to him in the loud place. He chirped and hopped out. Before exploring, he wanted to greet this new person. He jumped into her lap and then frantically climbed up onto her shoulders, meowling the whole time. After sniffing her hair, he decided that he liked her, so he banged his head into hers. She put her hand on him and he felt a little less frantic. He climbed down her back with only a few more meowls and then bolted across the room.

He approached one of the cats, sniffed her nose, and then batted a fake mouse at her. She batted it back and moved toward him in a friendly manner. This pleased him. He then went over to the other cat, who growled in a most intimidating fashion. This did not please him. He meowled and ran quickly to the person to ask more questions. Are you sure I'm in the right place? Is there, perhaps, somewhere else I am supposed to be? He was not convinced. The hand comforted him again and he settled down.

The person fed him and then let him take a nap in her lap. He woke up disoriented and full of even more questions. He decided to play some games with the friendly cat. They chased the fake mouse together until they both got tired. When he laid down, the friendly cat plopped down next to him and started licking his head. He closed his eyes and drifted off to sleep.

That night, the person put him in a new room. He saw food, water, a litter box, an object to climb on, and lots of soft pillows and blankets. Not a bad room. But then she left and closed the door. Little Claude was alone. All alone. He cried and scratched at the door, but the person did not return. He made himself into a tiny ball next to a pillow and cried himself to sleep. Finally, the next morning, he heard the person opening the door and prepared himself for action. As soon as she entered the room, he leapt onto her and climbed to her shoulders. She put her hand on him and he felt a little better. He tried to meowl his feelings to her but feared she did not understand.

He spent that day with the person and the friendly cat. They looked out various windows, played with toys, ate, and took naps. It was generally a good day. But then nighttime came, and again he found himself alone in the room. He was a very upset little Claude. He cried and cried and cried, but the person did not let him out until the next morning. Again, he meowled his concerns to her, but she did not understand.

Or did she? That night, after she put him in the room, she brought a cage in and set it down in the corner. Claude approached it cautiously. Inside, he saw the friendly cat. They touched noses through the bars of her cage. Claude liked her. He laid down next to her cage. Soon, he was sleeping peacefully.

* * *

Most cats will be very nervous when put in any new environment and will take time to adapt. Just like people, some cats are extroverts and some are introverts. Some thrive on social activity and some prefer less interaction. And then there's Claude. Claude must have a person or cat near him at all times or he becomes extremely agitated and anxious. It pains me to think now about how tortured he must have felt those first two nights when I left him alone. I thought he was just taking time to adjust to his new home, but the truth is that he cannot cope with reality alone. Fortunately, I was able to provide plenty of company. He has been with me for two years and has only been alone twice – both times because he sneaked into the bathroom and I closed him in there without being aware of it. His alarmed cries when he realized he was alone alerted me soon enough. If I want him out of a room and he doesn't want to come out, all I have to do is get everyone else out and close the door on him. Then I wait about 60 seconds and he starts pawing at the door to be released. Aside from making him dependent on social reassurance, Claude's anxiety manifests in a variety of other interesting ways. For instance, he is a very fastidious boy. I know that covering scents is instinctive behavior, but most indoor cats realize that they need not go to great lengths to cover their tracks to avoid predators. Claude, on the other hand, not only acts according to these instincts but takes them to a new level. He's like a person with obsessive-compulsive disorder checking to make sure a task has been done properly. He often goes into the litterbox right after someone else has used it and covers whatever is there even more. If he finds leftover food in anyone's dish, he will either eat it or cover it with something. If he finds a new blanket in the living room, he will drag it to the den and spend quite a bit of time arranging it how he likes it. The lesson I've learned from him is that every cat truly is an individual, with unique psychological and emotional needs. While there may be very good general advice available for new adopters, there's no one-size-fits-all for how to help a cat or kitten adjust to a new life in a new home.

* * *

October 5, 2022

Claude was now a year and a half old and had decided not to grow any bigger. He was not one bit embarrassed by his very small head. Now, some young cats go through a phase of having a head that looks too small for their body, usually because they have been eating so much that their bodies have fattened up before their heads have finished growing. Not Claude. Claude decided to keep his small head and narrow body because they go so well with his strong sneaking reflex. He instinctively slips past his person into any room, closet, cabinet, or box as soon as she opens it, regardless of whether he actually wants to be in it. His person finally learned to suppress her anti-sneaking reflex so that she would not keep accidentally almost closing a door on his tail.

Little Claude looks like the pet pet that he is. Today he has found his master and, after chasing him and rolling around with him, he has snuggled on top of him in the cat tree to take a well-earned nap.

* * *

A pet pet is a pet who has been adopted for the purpose of being a companion for another pet. I had taken in a kitten, Lionel, as a medical foster for the shelter and then decided a month later that I needed to keep him, even though he was annoying my two adult cats.

I figured that getting him his own pet would give the grown-ups some peace, so I adopted Claude to be Lionel's pet. I didn't introduce them right away because I wanted to be sure that Claude had adjusted to his new environment at least a little bit. When they first saw each other, Lionel did a lot of hissing, but Claude was eager to be friends. He was a very likeable pet, and he won Lionel over within a few days. Soon, the boys were taking turns chasing each other around the house and turning into a ball of cat. When they tired themselves out, they would sleep intertwined on the couch or the cat tree. It was true love. For anyone considering adopting a kitten, I would recommend adopting two together if possible. They will provide the kind of companionship to each other that people just can't offer, and they will not need as many toys because they'll entertain each other continually. Once a cat is an adult and has been living with a person for some time, the introduction of a new cat can present serious challenges. For more on that topic, see the comments after Athena's story.

* * *

December 5, 2022

Little Claude tries very hard to be a good boy, but sometimes he disobeys. One day, he was playing with the blinds and got himself all tangled up in the cords. His person asked him to stop and get down, but he did not want to stop. Instead, he tried to jump up to the top of the window but then he got really stuck. His person was suddenly angry. She untangled him and then yelled at him and said he could have gotten hurt. She yelled at Little Claude! How could she? He ran away as fast as he could, straight down the hallway, into the living room, around to the dining room, through the kitchen, over the counter, into the den, and then straight back down the hallway into the very same room he had just fled. He leapt into his person's arms. "I got yelled at!" he cried. "Comfort me!"

* * *

As most cat people know, disciplining cats is very tricky – and by "very tricky," I mean basically impossible. In general, yelling or using a loud, mean voice with your cat is a terrible idea – it will just create a state of fear and anxiety, will damage any bond that you've formed with your cat, and will not get the behavior that you want. However, yelling at a cat on those rare occasions when someone's life is in danger can be effective, especially if you almost never yell. For example, I once saw that one of my cats was about to step on the hot stove and I was across the room, so I yelled to scare him enough to stop him in his tracks so that I could run grab him before there was an injury. He was scared, I was scared, and I've never stepped away from a hot stove since then. Yelling worked. If a cat is fighting too rough with another cat, I might yell in a firm voice and, usually, the cats will stop, look at me, and then separate.

For regular fighting or bullying, though, yelling is not the answer. After living together peacefully for months, Lionel and Cleopatra became sworn enemies. I'm not sure why, but I suspect it happened after he decided to chase her and she fled. Why don't cats realize that the feline predatorial instinct is triggered by seeing an animal running away? I tried to explain this concept to Cleopatra: "How do you feel when you see a smaller animal running away from you? You want to run catch it, right? Because you are a cat. Now, if another cat is chasing you and you don't want him to identify you as prey, should you run? No. You should stand your ground. Same idea here. You're both cats." She didn't get it. The first couple of times that he chased her aggressively, I yelled. Then I decided that was bad. Then I tried clapping my hands loudly. Cats hate these types of sudden, obnoxious loud noises. The clapping startled both of them and shut down Lionel's attack mode. But by the fourth or fifth time I used the clapping, it had stopped working. They hated it, it made Cleopatra even more stressed out, and Lionel knew that nothing else would happen so he didn't stop his attacking behavior. So then I decided I would use SuperNanny's "naughty chair" time-out technique and pick Lionel up as soon as he lunged at Cleopatra and take him away to his room. I left him in his room alone for about 15 minutes and then went in to talk to him about his behavior, just like SuperNanny would. He was very sweet and seemed to purr his remorse and apologies to me. What didn't occur to me at first was that he had food in his room and did not actually dislike his room, so being sent there did not give him much reason to modify his behavior. I used this strategy once or twice per day at the first sign of aggression toward Cleopatra. After a couple of weeks, I realized that Lionel was associating attacking Cleopatra with getting to go to his food dish. He's the only one who doesn't finish his food all at once, so he often has left-overs available. Instead of just asking to be let back into his room, he would attack Cleopatra and I would then take him to his room, and he would eat. I had been outsmarted.

Cats will act like cats whether we like it or not, and we will act like people whether they like it or not. People need to adjust to cats rather than trying to discipline them. Some people use spray bottles to deter unwanted behavior, but I reserve this method to break up serious fights, not for issues like getting on the counter or scratching the couch. In fact, I don't use any method at all to stop cats from getting on the counter or scratching the couch. In my experience, cats will get on the counter and scratch the couch if they want to. If I don't want them to scratch certain items, I just put cardboard scratchers near those items and encourage them to use those instead. There are "keep away" products on the market, but I've never been motivated to try them.

* * *

Claude gazes admiringly at his own portrait

Lionel

Lionel has an ISFP - T personality type. Introverted but still adventurous, he needs both social time and alone time to flourish. He prefers the company of just one or two good friends and does not warm up to new people or cats easily. He can be unpredictable and likes to have the freedom to express himself however he pleases.

Lionel woke up feeling better. He had been so sick, with a stuffy nose and terrible headache. The last few days were a blur, but he remembered having to breathe out of his mouth and not wanting to eat any food at all. Now, he could breathe again, and he was a little hungry. When his person appeared at his door, he chirped at her happily. "I'm better today!" he exclaimed. He thought for a moment about how he could convey his feelings. He headbanged his person and then put his head down on the floor and flipped over backwards. "That was fun," he thought, and did it again. His person laughed at his somersaults and petted him, then hopped up on his bed and called him over. Lionel happily went to his person and snuggled against her. Then he put one arm on her shoulder and suckled on her neck for a little while. He felt so happy to be well again.

Soon, he heard Claude meowling outside his door and asked his person if he could go out and play. He had been stuck in his room for almost a week and suddenly wanted to leave. His person opened the door and Claude jumped on him. Lionel greeted his silly pet and then ran to the living room.

After a little while, his person took him back to his room and gave him some food. Lionel had forgotten that he was hungry. Now he remembered! He ate all of the food quickly and then pawed at the door to go back out to see his friends. His person let him out again, and this time she opened the door to the big room where Athena lived. Lionel chirped and trotted in. He liked that room because of the extra-long tunnel in it. He went through the tunnel and over to the window. He noticed that Athena was on her cat tree but he decided not to bother her. "Maybe I'll jump on her later," he thought. "For now I will play with these toys in the sun spot by the window."

Lionel watches Cat TV in bed as he recovers from an illness

* * *

I took Lionel in as a medical foster from the shelter. He was about three months old and had spent the last two weeks in a cage, medicated for coccidia and an upper respiratory infection. I carried him to my car without having gotten a good look at him, and when I opened the carrier door, our eyes met. Even though I think most cats are good-looking, I was surprised by just how cute he was. He was extremely cute. He seemed as pleasantly surprised as I was. He was instantly interested in forming a friendship. When I got him home, I let him out of the carrier onto the carpeted floor and he looked at me as if to say, "Wow, this is nice!" Then I proceeded to flea-comb him thoroughly, which I suppose he thought was a full-body massage. He purred and purred. Then I showed him the window and a little cat house, gave him some food, and left the room for about an hour. When I returned, he was exactly where I had left him. I got on the full-size bed and invited him up. He looked at me as if to say, "Oh boy, can I get on the bed?" So cute. He made biscuits on the bed while gazing lovingly into my eyes. I gave him a cat toy and he acted like it was the coolest thing he had ever seen. He jumped on and off the bed, chasing the toy and bringing it back up to me. That night, I slept on the bed with him and he continued to convey his sense of wonderment. At some point during the night, he snuggled up to me and began suckling on my neck. Like many cats who are separated from their mothers too young, he transferred his instinctive need to suckle onto a human. Thereafter, he suckled on my neck most days. Although it was quite slobbery and rather painful, I didn't have the heart to push him away because he seemed to need to do it and would always throw one arm over my shoulder, which was very endearing. He didn't stop until he was close to two years old.

I had fully intended to return Lionel to the shelter to be adopted by someone else once he had recovered from his infections, but I accidentally let him bond to me so strongly that he seemed virtually unadoptable in a shelter environment. I found out about this problem when I invited my mom (a very sweet, very small lady who loves cats and has probably never frightened an animal in her life) to come visit my precious foster kitty who was so loving. As soon as he saw her, he flattened his ears, began growling, and assumed not a defensive but an offensive posture. He was going to attack my little mom. When I took him back to the shelter, he was very hissy and scared. So I realized that if he were put back in the cat room, he would cower in the corner hissing at everyone. Not a good situation for a cat needing to be adopted. So, I have a piece of advice for people fostering kittens older than about 10 weeks: socialize them, but don't let them become so bonded to you and only you that they will not be attractive to future prospective adopters.

Kittens at shelters are commonly vulnerable to various viruses that cause upper respiratory infections, including herpesvirus and calicivirus. Once they have contracted the virus, they are likely to have stress-induced recurrences of symptomatic infection during their first year of life and, in some cases, for the rest of their lives. Lionel went through several rounds of it. After he recovered from the case that I was fostering him through, he went back to the shelter for neutering surgery and, a few days later, became sick again with a worse version of the original infection. This time, he got so bad I had to take him to the vet. He was breathing through his mouth and had refused to eat for more than 24 hours – both signs that a cat needs veterinary care immediately. They did a nebulized breathing treatment and prescribed new medications. He recovered within a week, but then a couple months later, a few days after I took him to the vet for his last round of vaccine boosters, he got sick again, so I concluded that he has a weak immune system and is prone to stress-induced viral upper respiratory problems and other infections. Fortunately, he slowly got stronger and eventually grew into quite a large, healthy cat.

Lionel

* * *

Chloe

Chloe has an ESFJ - T personality type. She is attentive to the needs of others, is known as the supportive one in her community, and often shows a true spirit of generosity. This personality is the most likely to trust completely.

At the age of about six months, Chloe found herself in a new place after several very confusing days in different cages in loud rooms. A person picked her up out of the box she was in and set her on a soft floor. She looked around calmly. She noticed a window, a tunnel, some toys, and two other cats in the room. She walked around a little and then greeted one of the cats. He was not much bigger than a kitten and seemed nice enough. The other cat, who was very skinny but obviously older, did not seem interested in interacting with anybody. Chloe went to the window and plunked herself down in front of it so that she could look outside. "This will do fine," she thought, and soon drifted off to sleep.

When she woke up, Chloe did not feel worried about her new situation. Curious, yes, but not worried. The person brought her food and she ate it happily. Then she watched the young cat as he played. She joined him in a few games. When night came, the person took the young cat to a different room, leaving her alone with the skinny cat. Chloe decided to introduce herself. The skinny cat growled, hissed, and raised its paw. Chloe stood still and scrunched her eyes closed, sensing what was about to happen. The skinny cat hit her in the face. Chloe stayed very still and quiet and waited for a moment before opening her eyes. Then she looked carefully at the skinny cat. "This is a scared girl," Chloe thought. "She's not mean. She's scared." Chloe walked slowly to the other side of the room and plunked herself down. She watched the scared, skinny cat for several minutes, and then the person returned to the room. The skinny girl let the person stroke her, which seemed to have a calming effect. Chloe decided to try introducing herself again. She approached more slowly this time, and the skinny cat growled but did not hiss. Chloe sat in front of her, touched her nose, and then began grooming the top of her head. "Maybe this will make her feel better," Chloe thought. The skinny cat did not try to hit her again. "We might not be friends," Chloe thought, "but there's no need to be enemies."

For the rest of the week, Chloe spent most of her time identifying places in the house that she liked and getting to know the other cats. As it turned out, there were three more cats besides the first two that she had met in the room. It was fine. She had no problems with any aspect of her new life here. For the most part, she did exactly as she pleased. For the first few nights, the person put her in a cage overnight so she couldn't go everywhere she wanted to, but she didn't really mind. The friendly young cat slept next to her cage and the person always let her out of the cage in the morning. It was fine.

As time passed, she began to understand everyone's personalities better. The friendly young cat had anxiety and lots of energy, which sometimes annoyed her a little. She soon learned that she could calm him down by grooming him, so if he became too annoying, she would simply walk over to him, put a paw on his head, and start grooming. Ears first, then top of head, then neck and shoulders. By the time she was finished, he was much more docile. The same technique worked with the skinny cat, who was very jumpy and sometimes growly. The orange cat and the big black cat noticed how she groomed the other two and started coming over to her to ask for head licks. They would just stick their head under her chin and wait. Chloe thought they were a bit presumptuous to expect that she would stop what she was doing and groom them every time they asked her to, but she did it anyway. It was fine. She liked to be surrounded by creatures who were content.

* * *

This story doesn't begin to capture the cuteness of little Chloe. Her genuinely compassionate attitude toward the others makes her unusual for a cat. Certainly, most cats show that they care about their friends, but Chloe has consistently demonstrated patience and kindness even toward cats who are not her friends. She sometimes gets tired of rough play and lets Claude or Lionel know that it's time to stop, but she never shows fear or meanness toward them.

Chloe's high degree of self-composure and complete lack of fearfulness also set her apart from most other cats. She has never shown any hesitation to interact with people. I can pick her up, put her in a cat carrier, and take her to the vet, and she doesn't seem to mind. At the vet, I open the cat carrier and she just looks calmly at the vet and allows herself to be handled. She is not even afraid of handymen. When a man was in the house using a loud drill on the floor, Chloe walked right up to him to say hi and see what was going on, while all five of the other cats cowered under the bed and behind the couch. She does not love to be picked up and hugged, but when she decides that she wants my attention, she will run to me at top speed, hop up next to me, and ask for a back scratch. If I stop sooner than she would like, she paws at me.

I would not be so surprised about Chloe's disposition if she had been raised in a loving home since kittenhood, but I adopted her from the shelter, where she had been designated as a barn cat. For this reason, I can only conclude that her personality is hard-wired from birth. Quite simply, Chloe trusts that the universe is a good and safe place and that she is exactly who she is supposed to be, where she is supposed to be. I have met happier cats and more affectionate cats, but I haven't met any cats who are more content or more self-assured than Chloe.

* * *

Cleopatra

Cleopatra has an INTP - T personality type. A logical thinker with a tendency to be reserved, she values her independence but needs to have contact with others. She can be impatient and quite demanding. She leans toward perfectionism, wanting everything arranged precisely as she thinks best.

Cleopatra had been left alone in the room for far too long. She had finished eating and had nothing else to do. She could hear the person interacting with the others and needed to know what they were doing. She scratched at the door. No answer. She reached under the door, grabbed it, and shook it as hard as she could. Nothing. She jumped up on the table near the door and then threw herself at the doorknob. No luck. She yowled. No response. Now she was getting angry at the person and wondered what could be the matter. She began pacing the room, and then her eyes lit on the cardboard scratcher that she often used to alleviate her anxiety. She ripped a big piece off of it and carried it in her mouth to the door. Then she dropped it and pushed it under the door and into the hallway. She repeated the process five or six times, making sure that each piece was at least a couple of inches long so that the person would be sure to see it. "Maybe the person's gone deaf," Cleopatra reasoned, "but surely she hasn't lost her sight also." Finally, the person opened the door and let her out. "What took you so long?" Cleopatra demanded. "Didn't you get my messages, you idiot? Can't you read?" Of course, Cleopatra had not actually written anything on the pieces of cardboard, as she felt that the message they conveyed was self-evident.

Cleopatra surveyed the living room and den and then hopped onto her usual perch. Still a bit angry, she continued to observe everyone's activities without participating. Slowly, her negative emotions dissipated, and she decided to hop down to play with Chloe, who was batting a ball around. Chloe was doing it wrong, so Cleopatra demonstrated the correct batting technique. Then she noticed the person watching. "Okay," Cleopatra said. "I forgive you. You may pet me." As a special favor, she even let the person pick her up and cuddle her. She was feeling much happier now.

* * *

When I adopted Cleopatra, I made some quick assumptions about her that turned out to be wrong. The shelter staff had put her in the barn cat program, probably because she was super skinny, missing a lot of fur, extremely skittish, and seemed like she might rip a person to shreds. I was really nervous letting her out of her cage, but I quickly realized that she was not truly feral. After I fed her and spoke softly to her, she hopped up onto a shelf above me and then jumped down directly onto my back as if to say hello. Then she came around to face me and shot her tail straight up in the air to indicate a willingness to be friends. She wanted me to pet her.

Cleopatra - skinny & scared in top 2 photos, looking better in bottom pic

So far, she was defying all of my expectations, but I continued to cling to the ideas I had already formed about her. I thought she would want a safe, solitary space away from everyone else, and when she growled at Chloe I became convinced that I would need to accommodate her separately. I set up a bedroom just for her, with a cat tree, blankets, cat beds, food, water, cat toys, and a covered litter box. That night, I left her alone in the room. She woke me up repeatedly with ridiculously loud yowling. Each time, I got up and went to see what she needed. I gave her more food, I petted her, I calmed her down. I figured she was just adjusting to her new home. In the morning, I saw that she had started tearing up the carpet from under the baseboards. I had to find heavy objects and mats to put over the places she had worked on so that she would not hurt herself on the sharp tack strips that she had exposed. The next night, I tried leaving her door open, so this time she yowled directly outside my door and ripped the carpet up in the hallway. I was beginning to get the feeling that she just wanted to be with me. I could not think of a solution because I did not want to betray Athena by letting a new cat into our sleeping room. The following nights, I left Cleopatra in her room with the door closed and just got used to being woken up periodically by her yowling. I put a cardboard scratcher in her room with the idea that she might be able to work on it instead of pulling up the carpet. In the mornings, I started to notice how anxious she was to leave her room right after finishing her breakfast. She didn't seem to love the other cats, but she wanted to be in the middle of the action. She would observe everyone from a safe distance and sometimes join in the games. I realized that she was very smart and very introverted but also needed to see everything that was happening. She did not need a safe space all by herself. She needed to be alone and together at the same time.

I changed the sleeping arrangements and put Claude and Chloe in her room with her at bedtime. They each had their own food dish, and I made sure that there were plenty of different places for them to sleep. Cleopatra claimed her spot at the top of the cat tree and didn't yowl once all night. In the morning, she seemed more relaxed. Claude and Chloe also seemed content. I guess the moral of this story is: don't make assumptions about what a new cat will need, want, and prefer. Also, vinyl plank flooring is a lot more practical than carpet if adopting or fostering animals.

* * *

Athena

Athena has an INTJ - T personality type. She is a strategic thinker, a thoughtful observer, and a bit of a loner. Often critical of others, she shows no need for companionship with other cats. Rationality and independence dominate her personality.

Athena was only five or six weeks old when she found herself alone, tossed on the side of a road in a residential neighborhood in Costa

Rica. She cried as loudly as she could for her mother, but to no avail. Finally, a huge creature appeared in response to her cries. The creature put its face close to hers, and Athena thought for sure she was about to be eaten. Instead, the creature lifted her up high into the air. "Put me down!!" screamed Athena. Slowly, the creature lowered her back down to the ground. Athena blinked. She knew she needed help. "Okay, pick me up!!" she screamed. The creature lifted her up again and stroked her fur gently. "No, put me down! Put me down!" Athena was shrill this time. The creature placed her back on the ground. She wanted to run away, but she was scared to be alone again. Something about this creature made her feel less scared. She reasoned that if it were going to eat her, it would have put her in its mouth already. "Okay, pick me up! Pick me up!" The creature picked her up and held her against itself. The creature was warm and soft, and Athena did not hate it. Athena decided to let the creature carry her around to look for her mother. They looked everywhere but finally gave up. The creature took Athena across the road and into a building. There, the creature gave her some milk and scrambled eggs. "Tasty," thought Athena. She didn't hate this creature at all. She fell asleep on its neck, just under its big non-pointy ear.

Athena agreed to live with the creature permanently. They spent all of their time together for weeks, but then one day, the creature left and did not return for many hours. Athena was worried. When the creature returned, she climbed up to its shoulder, sniffed its neck, and slapped it hard on the cheek, which made the creature laugh. Athena decided to make this a routine. Every day for the next few weeks, whenever the creature returned from wherever it had been, Athena would run as fast as she could up its body and onto its shoulder so that she could give it a good slap.

Athena loved chasing lizards and bugs. One day, she spotted a spider on a wall, but it was too high to reach. She leapt and stretched but couldn't quite reach it. Thinking quickly, she ran under the bed and retrieved her stuffed dog toy. She dragged it to the spot below the spider, stood on it, and then successfully launched herself up to catch her prey. She caught it, but it was larger than she had expected. Larger than her whole head, in fact. Suddenly, the creature appeared and made a loud noise, which startled her. The creature used a towel to grab the spider from her and then ran outside with it. That seemed unfair. Athena sulked and then bit the creature on its leg when it came back inside. The creature looked at her and said, "Tarantula!"

L - R: Athena at 6 weeks; Athena goes to work with the creature; Athena does her best Princess Diana imitation

A few days after the spider incident, Athena was exploring a room that had an opening to the sky above it. She watched as an object floated down and landed near her. Curious, she ran over to it and picked it up in her mouth. It was green and thin and a little crunchy on the edges. She dropped it and batted it around. She loved the way it moved. She wanted to share her excitement, so she carried this new object to the creature and dropped it at its feet. She looked up at the creature with love and wonder in her eyes. "You won't believe what I found!" she said. "Isn't it amazing?" The creature stroked her gently and congratulated her on her leaf. Athena realized that she loved the creature.

A couple of months later, Athena and the creature moved to a new place called Florida. It was similar to the other place, but instead of spiders there were cockroaches. One morning, during a heavy rain storm, many roaches came into the living area through a tiny crack by the window and Athena attacked them one by one. She ate part of one but did not like it much. Still, she loved catching them in her mouth before killing them. When the creature woke up and saw all the dead roaches smeared across the walls and floor, it picked Athena up, cuddled her, and began singing a song about how Athena was a hero. Athena felt proud of her work.

Sometimes, Athena needed the creature's help to catch the roaches. If one appeared on the ceiling, she would alert the creature, who would then grab an object such as a shoe. After locking eyes with Athena for a moment, the creature would swat the roach so that it would fall near Athena, who would always quickly catch it. Then the creature would sing sweetly to Athena. Athena felt happy to have the creature as a co-worker. They made a good team.

After a while, Athena and her creature left Florida and moved to a new place that was not as hot all the time. The floors were soft and, although there were no roaches to catch, there were lots of toys to amuse her. They lived happily together there for many months.

Then one day the creature brought a small black kitten into their home. Athena glared at the creature. "Why have you done this?" she asked. The creature played with the kitten, who hopped around stupidly. Athena hissed at it but it didn't seem to care. It started playing with all of her toys and then found her favorite ball and knocked it loudly into the walls so that it bounced all over the room. The creature seemed amused. Why would the creature like this obnoxious kitten? Athena left and went to a different room, hoping the creature would leave and take the kitten with it. Eventually, the creature took the kitten away.

The next day, Athena decided to show the creature that she could do everything that the kitten could do, so there was no need to have the kitten come live with them. Athena found the ball and knocked it so hard into the wall that it flew across the room. "See?" Athena said. "If you need somebody to do that for you, I can do it just fine." The creature cuddled Athena and told her that the kitten would not be coming to live with them.

But the creature wasn't telling the whole truth. A year later, Athena and the creature moved to a big new place and the kitten was there, but it had grown up into a big black cat with a silly white bib. It had its own room, but Athena did not approve of the situation. Every morning it would stick its paws under her door. Ridiculous.

As the days went by, Athena became accustomed to the new place and decided not to growl at the stupid cat when it came to the door. One day, she decided to bat its paws. It was kind of fun. The next day, the cat pushed a toy under the door toward her. Athena swiftly grabbed it, but the cat reached under again with its enormous paws and swiped it back. At first, Athena was angry, but then she realized that she was enjoying herself. This is a pretty fun game, she thought. Maybe the cat is not all that bad.

Every morning and evening, Athena would play with the cat under the door, until one day the creature opened the door so that they could see each other face to face. Athena sniffed the cat's nose and then slapped its cheek. It was a stupid big boy cat. Obnoxious. However, she decided to watch him for a while instead of running back into her room.

Athena got used to the morning routine – eat food and play with her creature, then play under the door with the cat. Sometimes, the creature left the door open and played with both of them. Athena went to the cat's room and saw his tunnel. She watched the cat run through it. Sometimes, the creature tossed treats around and both she and the cat would run to get them.

It occurred to Athena that she and the cat had a number of shared interests. It even seemed possible that she had more in common with the cat than she did with the big creature. Athena quickly dismissed these thoughts, however, as she much preferred the company of the creature to that of the cat.

About a year later, Athena and the creature and the cat all moved to a new place, and not many months after that, an orange kitten came to stay with them. At first, Athena was merely aware of the kitten's presence in a closed room but never really saw him. One day, though, the creature brought the orange guy out into her living area and let him run around. He ran right toward her and had the audacity to throw his little arms around her neck. Athena hissed at him vigorously. The creature put him back in his room. Not long after, unfortunately, three more cats came to the house and were split up into different rooms. Athena had no idea what was going on.

The days went by and Athena wondered why there were so many cats. Slowly, the creature brought all of them together in her living space. Athena noticed that the new cats entertained each other and mostly left her alone. She decided that she was okay with the situation since the creature kept them away from her. Still, she wistfully remembered the days of living alone with the creature and wished that these new cats would disappear.

One day, Athena fell asleep in her usual spot next to the creature on the couch and woke up to find that she was sandwiched between two sleeping cats who had nestled against her. She sighed and went back to sleep, knowing that the creature was still there and would protect her. At least the stupid cats were warm.

In the months and years that followed, Athena became comfortable with the new situation but never accepted the other cats as real friends. The creature was her only true friend. The orange cat always seemed to want to fight or play with her, but the others mostly respected her space. One cat – a small gray fellow that the creature called "Claude" –

sometimes came to her and tried to butt her with his head. He looked at her with silly googly eyes and sometimes laid down in front of her. The creature always stroked him and said that he was trying to tell Athena that he loved her. It was no use, though. Athena did not speak cat. She only understood the creature's language.

* * *

Since I adopted Athena when she was barely six weeks old, I kept her with me at all times for the first few weeks. My boss let me bring her to work with me, and she slept on my lap or in the crook of my elbow for most of each day for the first week. She soon got to the age of romping, so I enlisted my co-workers to supervise her when I was busy. When she was ten weeks old, I had to start leaving her at my apartment alone but would rush home at lunch to see her. As a result of all of our togetherness, we formed a strong bond.

Anyone adopting a lone kitten really needs to have time to devote to the vulnerable creature during such an impressionable time of life. The rewards are amazing: the kitten will love you, trust you, show loyalty to you, and delight you as you watch all of the stages of development.

Anyone who wants to enjoy the companionship of more than one cat should really consider adopting two kittens together. If a lone kitten is separated from littermates and the mother very early, he or she will likely not understand basic feline communication and will probably be distrustful of cats. Athena is the only one of my cats who does not seem to have any idea what other cats' signals mean. If they come too close to her, she assumes a defensive posture immediately. Claude behaves perfectly appropriately for someone who wants to come in peace – he approaches gently, lowers his head and looks down, lies down in front of her in a show of submission, tries giving her a friendly head butt – but Athena does not know how to interpret his cat messages. She acts no differently than she does when Lionel comes running at her from behind and tries to throw his arms around her.

Patience is the key to introducing new cats to each other. Suddenly thrusting a cat into another cat's living space will usually result in high stress levels for everyone involved. Most vets and cat people suggest starting with cats in separate rooms, behind closed doors for a couple of days so that they can sense each other's presence in the house. Giving each one an item of clothing or fabric with the other's scent on it might also be a good idea. The next step is to encourage them to play under a door if possible. They can use paws and toys to get to know each other a bit. After a few days of this activity, a person can carefully open the door while they are playing and let them sniff noses. Ideally, they will not freak out. Their interaction will likely need to be limited for the first few days and then gradually increased. They should be supervised until they can be trusted not to hurt each other. Feeding them treats together as a routine can help them associate togetherness with a positive outcome. Cats are generally quick to detect a routine, so they might soon look forward to their time together if they know that they will also get a tasty reward.

If one cat has already bonded with a person alone, the person should take care to demonstrate loyalty to the first cat while introducing new ones into the household. I made sure to show Athena that I would always take her side in any dispute and shoo away any cat who made her uncomfortable, so she soon became more confident around the new cats – as long as I was not far away. If a cat started bugging her, she would run to me, I would praise her and sympathize with her, and she would snuggle up next to me for a while. I think the person should also be sure to reserve some time every day to spend alone with just the original cat. Athena sleeps in my bed with me every night and the others sleep in their own rooms.

* * *

Clouseau

Clouseau has an ISFP - T personality type. Mostly introverted but still appreciative of company, he values his time alone in his room as well as his time with the other members of the family. He is generally obedient but gets fussy if he can't express himself.

Clouseau was bored, but he didn't dare move. His mother had placed him between his brother and a cold metal wall and had given him strict instructions to stay quiet and not go anywhere. He was getting hungry and was tired of being wedged up against his anxious brother. Suddenly, the ceiling above him lifted into the air and he could see the outside world. A giant hand came swiftly toward him and snatched him up along with his brother. Clouseau was curious. Whose hand was this? He looked into the eyes of a big animal but was not afraid. Then two more of these animals appeared and took turns holding him. His brother cried, but Clouseau did not. These animals seemed okay, and they were certainly more interesting than his brother. Finally, his mom appeared and the animals set him down. His brother ran frantically to their mother and began nursing, but Clouseau trotted around and found some food that he saw one of the big animals put in a dish. He decided to eat the food instead of joining his brother. His brother was such a big baby.

A couple days later, Clouseau saw one of the big animals again. "Hi," he said. "Remember me?" The hand came down and picked him up. "It's just me," Clouseau said. The hand stroked him for a while before setting him back down. He romped off to play in the leaves.

A few weeks later, Clouseau found himself picked up by the hand again. This time, they left the outside world and entered a big house. Clouseau saw interesting items everywhere. He ran from one place to the next. He chased a ball, he picked up a fake mouse, and he climbed up onto a chair. Then he found a dish of food and water. Clouseau liked this place! He decided that he would be happy to stay inside.

* * *

Clouseau is Cassie's son, which also makes him the nephew of Bright Eyes and Beauty.

Feral moms often leave their kittens inside cars while they go off to hunt or to take a break. Sometimes the kittens are plainly visible when the hood is opened, but other times they are squeezed deep inside the works of the car or even inside a bumper. The moms command them to stay put, and they do. People who live in areas where there could be feral kittens should always pop the hood and slam it loudly before starting the engine to give the kittens time to leap out.

Kittens that appear to be younger than 8 weeks old should be left alone to be cared for by the mother. Sometimes well-intentioned people find tiny kittens and grab them and take them to a shelter. In most cases, the mother will come back looking for these kittens and will be distraught when she can't find them. The kittens themselves will not survive if a person is not available to immediately begin bottle-feeding them. Tiny kittens shouldn't go more than three or four hours without food. Even if the labor-intensive, round-the-clock feeding schedule for kittens can be followed, the kittens will not be as likely to become healthy adults as they would have been with their mother's milk. For these reasons, people who find little feral kittens should give the mother a chance to reappear and take care of them before assuming that they need to be rescued. If possible, the people should check on the kittens quietly and frequently or use a camera to monitor the area and see if the mother comes for them. If she does, then the people could consider setting up a safe, enclosed cat bed or shelter that the mother might decide to use. Only after the kittens have reached at least six weeks of age should they be caught. Of course, by then, they will be more difficult to catch, so trapping will probably be necessary. Using a drop trap could be a good way to trap the kittens and the mom at the same time. Then the kittens could be adopted and the mother could be spayed and released if she is truly feral. Local trap-neuter-release organizations can sometimes offer traps, assistance, and advice. Many of these groups of kind people have made helpful videos and websites that can be found easily online.

Distinct personality traits can be observed in kittens starting as young as two or three weeks. The extreme differences in kittens from the same litter can sometimes be explained by the fact that littermates can actually have different fathers, but even siblings with the same fathers can have completely different personalities and temperaments. Some might be easygoing like Clouseau and allow themselves to be picked up, while others might hiss and spit violently at people, and still others might simply flee as fast as they can. Clouseau's brother was feral and only happy outdoors. He would have been miserable if we had forced him inside.

Top left: Clouseau shares the couch with Lionel; Top right: Clouseau relaxes in his favorite pose; Bottom: Clouseau likes little Chloe, who is also a tuxedo cat

* * *

A Little More About Kittens

If at all possible, kittens should stay with their mother for 8 - 12 weeks. In the natural order of things, kittens will be with littermates most of the time during their first two or three months of life. They will learn how to play with each other, and the mother will correct their behavior.

If adopting a single kitten younger than this age, be prepared to give him or her frequent attention, as it would not be developmentally normal for the kitten to be completely alone. The kitten will need to be handled and supervised carefully. Kittens do bite and play rough, so a person will need to find ways to gently correct and redirect their behavior to prevent them from getting into the habit of biting people's hands and fingers too hard. It's tempting to play with the cute little kitten and let him or her bite you playfully, but it's usually best not to encourage this behavior; it's certainly not fair to allow it up to the point of being bitten hard and then to suddenly yell at the kitten or try to discipline it. If hand-feeding, remember that the kitten does not understand how to *not* bite any part of a person's hand while eating the food off of it. Several times, I have found out the hard way that kittens can accidentally bite clean through the fleshy part of a finger with their razor-sharp little kitten/shark teeth.

Prospective adopters of young kittens should seriously consider adopting two littermates together. They will actually be easier to care for, as they will have each other to play with and will usually sleep snuggled together for comfort. Cats are social beings, and most indoor cats will benefit from the companionship of another cat who has been a friend since kittenhood.

* * *

Bright Eyes

Bright Eyes has an ISFJ-T personality type known as "The Defender." She is introverted, sensing, feeling, judging, and turbulent. Like most reserved personality types, she takes her time to accept a new person or cat but can eventually sustain well-developed relationships. Bright Eyes is loyal, supportive, and reliable, but she does tend to take things personally, and she struggles with change.

When Bright Eyes woke up, it seemed a day like any other at first, but she soon sensed that her person was behaving strangely. She had grown accustomed to the tone of voice that her person used every morning when presenting the food, and today it seemed . . . different. "Here's yours, Bright Eyes," her person said – the words were the same as always, yet the attitude was not. Bright Eyes looked at the food and could clearly see that it was not the usual amount. She shot a quick glance at her person to indicate that she had detected the change instantly. Again, she could feel an unusual emotion radiating from her person.

"It's guilt!" Bright Eyes suddenly realized. "She is going to starve me and she feels guilty about it!"

Bright Eyes took a small bite and then thought of her poor babies who would not get enough to eat today. She walked off to retrieve both of them. She brought first one and then the other, and she laid them next to the food dish. She looked up at her person to say, "It's fine if you want to starve *me*, but think of the babies! The babies are hungry!"

The babies laid there, motionless as always since they were actually little stuffed cat toys. After allowing them sufficient time to help themselves, Bright Eyes resumed eating her paltry serving and finished quickly. Entirely dissatisfied, she marched away, leaving the babies behind so that they would be able to lick the dish clean if they suddenly came to life.

Bright Eyes knew she was fat. Her person regularly addressed her with words like "my big girl" and "my round one." She didn't think, though, that there was any need to lose weight. She was 8 years old and perfectly entitled to some mature weight gain. She thought exercise was goofy, and she watched Peppermint and Miss Marple run around chasing toys and laser beams in a most undignified and chaotic manner. She found herself somewhat curious about the toys' movements but never felt motivated to join in the fray.

A caretaker at heart, Bright Eyes decided to set aside her disappointment and go check on her person. Maybe her person was having some kind of trouble that prevented her from providing the usual amount of food. Bright Eyes loved sitting in her person's lap and gazing into her eyes. Today would be no different, despite the alarming breakfast situation. She hopped up onto her person's lap and studied her face. Sometimes she worried about her person and could tell when she was not feeling well. On these occasions, she tried to devote extra time to snuggling with her. Today, she decided that she would just take a short nap and think about the possibility of a larger-than-usual lunch.

Lunchtime came surprisingly late, but this time the dish was about as full as usual. "Okay," Bright Eyes thought, "I suppose we're getting back to normal." She made sure to let her babies have a chance to eat before polishing off the contents of the dish and then proceeding to her after-lunch room. In this room, she could look out the window and doze on and off while awaiting the arrival of possum. Possum was a funny-looking creature with an exceptionally long nose and tail. Bright Eyes herself had only a bobtail and found possum's long, skinny tail rather fascinating. It looked so much like a snake that it sometimes made her want to cackle a predatory cackle, but she refrained. She felt it important to maintain a sense of dignity at all times. Since she knew that she could not actually attack possum's tail, which was on the other side of the window, she did not want to give the appearance of thinking that she could. She always thought other cats looked foolish cackling at outdoor creatures that they could not possibly get their paws on.

Dusk fell and Bright Eyes grew more alert. Right on time, possum appeared. She watched him approach the rocky area under the window where her person had left some type of food. He was not a fastidious eater like Bright Eyes, and she marveled at the bits of food that he left scattered around. Wasteful, she thought. After a while, possum wandered off and Bright Eyes got up to stretch. She looked around to see what Peppermint was doing and realized that he was eating a treat on the kitchen floor. A treat? Where was her treat? Where was her person? Actually, wasn't it dinner time?

Confused, Bright Eyes went looking for her babies and soon found them not far from where she had left them. She carried them one at a time to the feeding area and gently placed them on the mat where her food dish should have been. Then she hopped up on her cat tree to watch and wait.

Finally, her person appeared and said the magic words: "Time for dinner, pretty girl." Bright Eyes hopped down from her perch and came eagerly to the food dish, not even giving her babies a chance to arise from their perpetual slumber. She gobbled the food quickly and was finished sooner than she would have expected. She looked around for her person, who was nowhere in sight.

Bright Eyes marched into the living room in search of her person but only found Shadow and Peppermint. She paced for about a minute before lying down to conserve her energy. Perhaps she was too big, after all.

Her person came around the corner soon enough, and Bright Eyes locked eyes with her silently. "I'm sorry, pretty girl," her person said, "But you've got to lose a bit of weight. You're going to the vet soon and we don't want another bad report."

Bright Eyes was not sure she could take this double dose of bad news. Forced weight loss *and* a visit to the vet? It was all too much. Bright Eyes sulked back to her own bedroom, climbed into her favorite cat bed, put her head down, and closed her eyes. Maybe her person would forget about this whole plan tomorrow and go back to the usual food routine.

* * *

Indoor cats can gain weight easily, which can lead to health problems including diabetes. This problem is often caused by feeding too much dry food or leaving a full bowl of dry food out all day. Wet food generally has fewer calories bite for bite and, according to many vets, is a better choice for most cats. Personally, I feed a combination of wet and dry on a regular feeding schedule, and I never leave food out after feeding time is over.

Unfortunately, once cats become quite fat, the options for achieving weight loss are limited, and people should never make a sudden change or withhold food. A slight, gradual decrease in daily quantities is usually best, and consulting a vet about food choices and routines is always advisable. Cats' bodies are unable to mobilize stored fat in the same way that humans' bodies do, so their livers can fail (hepatic lipidosis) if they go too long without food or face too much caloric restriction. While overweight human bodies would be more likely to survive a period of famine than underweight human bodies, overweight cat bodies could actually be the first to die of starvation, before normal-weight cat bodies would. In fact, there have been many reports of cats experiencing irreversible liver failure that began as a result of going without food for as little as 48 hours.

* * *

Peppermint

Peppermint as an ENTJ - T personality type. Strong-willed, self-confident, and dominant, he is the one that others look to for approval. He is slow to yield and generally uninterested in considering the perspectives of others. Still, as an extrovert, he enjoys being among a group, provided he can maintain his command post.

Peppermint walked into the living room, saw the pile of wrapped boxes, and knew there was going to be a party. How exciting! Peppermint loved a celebration. He saw his dad sitting at the table eating lunch. He looked around to see if his mom was in sight. The coast was clear. He hopped up onto the table and headbanged his dad's shoulder. His dad stroked him and offered him a bite of food. Peppermint sat down on the table and watched his dad eat and read. Suddenly, his mom appeared around the corner. Peppermint stood up defiantly. "Dad said I could be here!" he exclaimed. His mom matched his energy. "Peppermint, get down!" she said. "You know you're not supposed to be on the table!" Yes, Peppermint knew that was her rule, but he strongly disagreed with it. He decided to get down this time, but only because he wanted to prepare himself for the party.

Peppermint picked a spot on the couch near the presents and began grooming himself. He groomed and groomed, paying particular attention to his fancy tail. He was fully aware of the fact that he had the nicest tail of all. He used it to welcome people to his home, holding it straight up at first and then waving it slightly to and fro. How could anyone not admire this tail? It was spectacular.

Soon enough, people began arriving at the front door. Peppermint trotted back and forth to greet everyone and then led them into the living room full of gifts. Once everyone had settled in, the real fun began. As the gifts were opened, the wrapping paper was tossed into a box. Peppermint pounced into the box and sat on some of it, then batted the incoming pieces into the air. Soon, more empty boxes appeared. Peppermint jumped from one to the other. He knew that the people were watching him, so he put on a nice performance to entertain them. He wondered if anyone noticed any of his cat friends. Peppermint himself didn't even know or care where they were, so he assumed that none of the guests cared either. When the party was over, Peppermint proudly bid each guest farewell.

* * *

Peppermint has always been the ambassador cat who wants to host every party but is not very considerate of the other cats. He fancies himself king of the house and loves people and their visitors but shows less regard for his cat friends. He requires them to submit to his will and has a history of rejecting feline newcomers outright. He is a classic alpha.

Cats will often figure out how to play their people off of each other. They know very well what different people like, and they understand how to appeal to different personalities. Just like children, they can sense when one parent is more permissive than the other and will use this knowledge to their advantage at every opportunity.

* * *

Miss Marple

Miss Marple has an INFP - T personality type. Although outwardly reserved and unassuming, she has a strongly imaginative inner life, full of daydreams. She can be sensitive and emotional, and she generally seeks peace. She responds to artistic stimuli, which likely appeal to her creative side.

Miss Marple woke up about an hour before dawn, as usual, and looked around for her favorite toy, which she quickly realized was not on the bed. She paid no mind to the soft wincing sound she heard as she walked across her person, and she jumped to the floor with a thud. She was on a mission and did not wish to be distracted. After spotting the toy across the room, she retrieved it and carried it in her mouth to the window. There, she tossed the toy in the air and batted it around while also watching for any activity outdoors. This was her favorite time of day. One by one, her friends came to join her, and by dawn, they were all at the window together. She tried to engage the others in play, but they mostly just watched her and looked out the window. She didn't mind putting on a bit of a show. She had been working on her skills with this particular toy for a long time now and felt a sense of pride in her abilities. She could toss it quite high in the air and then smack it fairly far with her paw as it was falling.

Once it was fully daylight, Miss Marple looked around for her person. She knew it was breakfast time and hoped that her person had gotten up already to prepare the food. Miss Marple decided to go to the feeding area and wait. Soon enough, her person appeared and set a dish down in front of her. Miss Marple ate quickly and then went to see if perhaps she could gobble up any of her friends' food before her person noticed. No luck. Well, maybe she could try again at lunch. In the meantime, Miss Marple decided to go curl herself up in her favorite cat tree and take a nap.

* * *

Although many domestic and feral cats are active throughout the night, they are not categorized as nocturnal. Rather, cats are called "crepuscular," meaning that they are most active at dusk and dawn. I have noticed that extremely cold temperatures in the winter will interfere with this natural tendency, as outdoor cats will stay in their warm places until the sun comes out or even a little later; otherwise, though, my observations have generally confirmed the validity of the crepuscular categorization. Most people who let their cats sleep in their bedrooms with them will also be able to confirm that cats become active at or a little before dawn.

Cats have excellent vision in low-light conditions, and they seem to be aware that most other creatures have inferior visual ability in these circumstances. If cats seem bolder in dim lighting or in the dark, it's probably because they are confident that they have the advantage. People are afraid of the dark for good reason; cats are brave in the dark for equally good reason. Unfortunately, outdoor cats are not invincible at night and can still become prey to bigger, faster animals, especially coyotes and packs of dogs.

* * *

Shadow

Shadow has an ISFJ - T personality type. Introverted and observant, he is practical in an understated way. He can be relied on to do his share, but he does not need to take credit for accomplishments. He is quietly loyal and appreciates predictable behavior in those around him.

Shadow knew he was a creature of habit and he liked it that way. At the moment, he was in his favorite position, lying on his back in a sunspot with his front paws resting comfortably on his chest. He knew that a couple of his friends were in the same room, but they would not bother him if he drifted off to sleep. In about an hour, his person would be coming into the room with food. He would happily eat it and then go wander downstairs. He would look out the windows facing the back yard for about 15 minutes and then would go peer out the window overlooking the side garden for about the same amount of time. Next, he would go to the garage and check behind the boxes and bins. He wasn't quite sure what he was looking for, but he always needed to have a look anyway.

Shadow always let his people extend their hands to him so that he could sniff them. If they tried to pet, stroke, or cuddle him, he would bite them. He was very consistent so that there could be no misunderstanding. He observed his cat friends being petted all the time but did not see why they liked it so much. Shadow loved his people, but there was no need for them to put their big hands all over him.

* * *

When I first met my mom's cat Shadow, I asked her if I could pet him.

"Sure!" she said. So I slowly reached down to pet his head gently and he bit me very, very hard.

"Thanks, Mom!" I said. "He just put a hole in my hand."

"Well, that's our Shadow!" she laughed.

I suppose she thought that I was asking for permission rather than advice when I asked her if I could pet him. I've gotten to know Shadow better since our first painful meeting and have come to appreciate his ways. He was born feral, and my mom adopted him when he was still a kitten. He let her handle him when he was a little fellow, but as he grew older, his feral tendencies manifested clearly. He's not truly feral or even semi-feral, but I would say he's definitely at least a quarter feral. I have joked with my mom that if Shadow outlives her, her last act on earth may have to be dragging herself off of her deathbed to go grab him and put him in his carrier, because nobody else is going to be able to catch him and pick him up.

Establishing routines for cats will help maintain household peace and order and will especially help foster a sense of well-being in cats who have the wild streak in them. Cats figure out human routines quickly and establish their own, and they rely on the predictability of those routines to feel at ease each day. Disruptions will produce anxiety. Most cats can tell time very well and will remind their people if they are late for anything.

* * *

Claudia

Claudia has an ISFJ - T personality type and stands ready to protect her beloved people. Full of affection and quick to show how grateful she is to be loved and fed, she is eager to fight off any feline intruder with a startling amount of aggression for an elderly cat.

Claudia was not sure how she had ended up outside in the heat, so she was pleased when she stumbled upon a house with a shady area and a giant water dish. She drank her fill and then plunked herself down. Soon, a lady came out of the house and noticed her. Claudia was nervous and retreated behind some bushes, where she watched with great interest as the lady put a dish down on the ground and then went back inside the house. Claudia waited a few minutes and then walked over to check out the dish. It was food! What a nice surprise! Claudia ate it all quickly and returned to her spot in the bushes.

For the next several days, Claudia stayed in that spot, coming out twice a day to eat the food that the lady brought her. Finally, she decided to approach the lady and offer her friendship. Happily, the lady returned her friendly feelings. Just a couple of days later, the lady brought Claudia inside her house and gave her a nice, cool place to sleep and eat. Claudia purred and purred.

In the weeks that followed, Claudia met other people and liked them all. She was quite satisfied with her new living situation, until one day the lady and another person brought a big cat into the room. At first, Claudia did not notice the cat, but when she did, she was positively furious. She lunged at the cat, intending to kill it, but the person restrained her and then the lady took the cat away. The lady apologized to Claudia, but Claudia was confused. Why hadn't the lady let her kill the cat so that the house would be safe again?

A few days later, when the lady opened the door to her room, Claudia saw a different cat out in the hallway. She lunged at the door to kill the cat and save her lady, but the lady quickly closed the door and prevented Claudia from reaching the cat.

Claudia was confused. Clearly, the lady had a real cat problem, and Claudia was ready and willing to help her eliminate it. Why wouldn't the lady let her do her job?

* * *

Claudia is an elderly, declawed, polydactyl cat who somehow found my mom, who already had four cats. After my mom brought her inside, we wanted to introduce the cats to each other slowly, so we allowed them to be on opposite sides of a door for many days, with my mom's cats sniffing and pawing under the door. We later realized, though, that Claudia was almost totally deaf and had reduced smelling capacity, so she was never aware of the other cats outside her door. When we brought the gentle Bright Eyes into her room, Claudia was caught off guard and completely freaked out. If I had let her go, I think she would have killed poor Bright Eyes, despite being a very senior cat with no claws. I believe that Claudia is past the point in life when she could adapt to a new situation with other cats, so she will have her own room for the rest of her days. She loves my mom and seems quite content with her situation, as long as she cannot see any of the other cats.

* * *

BONUS CAT

Front Porch Guy

Front Porch Guy has an as-yet undetermined personality type but shows signs of being an ENFP, an ESTP, or an ESFP. He's definitely an extrovert and has an adventurous spirit.

Front Porch Guy was wandering around the neighborhood in the wee hours of the morning when something caught his eye: there were cats in a yard behind a fence. He trotted over to the fence to peer in. He counted at least four cats and sensed that there were more (and he was right). He tried to find a way to get over the fence, but something at the top made it very difficult for him. He gave up and contented himself with watching. One of the cats spotted him and approached with a floofed tail. Front Porch Guy wanted to show that he was not easily intimidated, so he let out a yowl that sounded ferocious enough to scare away a wolf. To his surprise, the approaching cat seemed undeterred. Front Porch Guy yowled some more, experimenting with different pitches. Suddenly, he heard a noise at the front of the house. A person had come outside and was talking to him. Front Porch Guy felt nervous and decided to run for cover under a nearby truck.

About half an hour later, Front Porch Guy got up the nerve to return to the house with all the cats. He cautiously approached the front porch and saw that there was fresh food and water in a dish there. He ate it quickly and then looked in the windows. More cats! He went from window to window and saw a different cat every time he looked inside. Front Porch Guy felt that he belonged at this house. But he could not find a way inside either the house or the yard.

The next day, the house pulled Front Porch Guy back to it like a magnet. Instead of visiting after midnight, he arrived around 7:00 pm. Some of the cats behind the fence saw him right away and yowled at him. The person soon appeared, and this time he saw her set a dish of food down. He waited for her to leave and then ate heartily. He felt happy but still had a nagging sense that he needed to find a way to join the others. Was this not his obvious destiny?

* * *

There will always be more cats waiting to meet their cat people, and vice versa.

11

A Philosophical Dialogue

Setting: The Patio. A group of both indoor and outdoor cats has gathered around Athena, who is on the upper perch of a cat tree and is speaking to all.

Athena: Let us now consider the topic of free will. Do we have free will? Or are our actions simply determined by instinct or some other force?

Cleopatra: Of course we have free will. We make our own choices. And yet the possibilities are limited by outside forces that restrain us.

Princess: The fence is the outside force that prevents us from exercising our free will.

Cleopatra: I don't know about the fence, but I would say that doors definitely act as a barrier to the exercise of free will.

Athena: Let's imagine that all the doors are open and the fence has fallen down. Now what? Do we have free will? Or do we act only according to instincts over which we have no control? Are all of our actions predetermined because we are cats?

Claude: What are instincts? I do what I do because I want to.

Lionel: Me too.

Chloe: Sometimes I'm not sure why I do what I do. For example, sometimes I jump on top of the refrigerator and start meowing at the ceiling. I don't know why.

Claude: I guess maybe I do things I don't understand also. Yesterday I woke up from a nap in the living room and suddenly flew as fast as I could through the kitchen and down the hallway. When I got to the end of the hall, I stopped and stared. "Why am I here now?" I asked myself. I didn't know. So I just went back into the living room.

Chloe: Sometimes when I'm eating cardboard, I think to myself that I should stop because it doesn't taste good and the texture is weird, but then I can't make myself stop. I just keep eating it and eating it. I spit most of it out, but still . . . why can't I just leave it alone?

Princess: I frequently slap cats and people when they haven't done anything to me. I don't know why. Sometimes I'll just look at someone and think, "I should slap you." Then I do.

Sibling: Sometimes I eat a lot of grass really quickly when I know it's going to make me vomit. Then I vomit. I don't know why I do that so often. I don't actually like vomiting. Who does?

Martha: Sometimes if I see someone else running, then I start running, but I don't know why we're running and I don't know where we're going.

Duchess, Cassie, and Beauty: ***(exchanging nods)*** Same!

Clouseau: Last week I got angry at the rug in my room and flipped it around until it was bunched up in the corner. It took me a long time. But I don't like the wood plank floor any better than the rug, so I have no idea why I did that.

Athena: So most of us can admit that we don't always act as a result of conscious decisions and free will but, rather, out of sudden impulses that we may not understand at the time. Cleopatra, how about you?

Cleopatra: I agree that all of you behave in a manner that indicates a certain level of subjugation to base and inexplicable instincts or impulses. Not me, though. I act according to a thoughtful decision-making process.

Athena: All right, we'll take you at your word. Lionel, how about you? Have you reconsidered your original stance?

Lionel: No.

Athena: Okay, so now

Lionel: Wait. Yesterday I bit my own tail really hard. It hurt. I don't know why I did that. Does that count?

Athena: Yes. So now we must ponder whether we exhibit free will some of the time. What do you think?

Lionel: I use my free will to make choices most of the time.

Cleopatra: If something like a door or Person is preventing me from doing what I choose to do, I continue to make choices. No creature is free from barriers and limitations.

Athena: So you're saying that if you want to leave your room but the door blocks your exit, then you choose what else to do in the room.

Cleopatra: Yes, obviously.

Athena: But couldn't we also argue that your actions are not the result of free will but, rather, of determinism? An outside force such as the person has chosen when the door will open and when the door will close. If the door is closed when you want to leave the room, you stay in the room. The choice of activities is limited to what is in the room. And you did not choose what is in the room – the person chose what is in the room. So, to some extent, your actions have been predetermined.

Cleopatra: You are undermining my sense of personal agency.

Athena: We are merely trying to understand the nature of our own behavior as cats. Perhaps it would help us to consider the behavior of other creatures. What can be said of the actions of Person? Do people have free will or are they, too, acting according to instincts beyond their control? Are their actions also heavily predetermined?

Duchess: The man who lives on the other side of the fence uses many machines that are so loud! He cuts the grass, he cuts the trees, he blows leaves around the yard, he turns on other machines with wheels and sits on them. Are the machines making him turn them on? How could he be choosing to make so much noise all the time? I can't believe it's free will.

Claude: Maybe he does it because he likes to use loud machines.

Clouseau: But he probably doesn't know *why* he likes to use loud machines.

Chloe: So he does it because he can't stop himself.

Beauty: He should rest more. He's not very good at resting.

Martha: That's true. He is constantly busy. But have you noticed that the people who live on the other side of the yard are more leisurely? They play music and eat delicious-smelling food outside. They must choose to relax, right?

Beauty: But if the loud machine man is bad at resting, maybe the other people are bad at working. The people act the way they do because they can't help themselves, not because they make lots of conscious decisions.

Athena: So can we say that behavior is predetermined by individual personality? Or by species-specific instincts and impulses? Or by forces outside the individual's control?

Claude: I get it! You're saying it's a combination of factors!

Athena: I merely pose the questions.

Chloe: Athena is suggesting that there's no such thing as pure free will for any creature. Everyone's actions are at least partly predetermined by something other than deliberate choice.

Lionel: What about Person?

Claude: I love Person.

Clouseau: Me too. Lap time is my favorite.

Athena: I love Person, too. The question is this: Does she act only according to free will? She brought some of us into her house, right? That was her choice, not ours, right? And the others of us here were brought to her yard, right? You guys didn't walk here on your own.

Princess: No! She brought me in a cage in a car. I was furious!

Cassie: Me too!

Sibling: Same.

Lionel: But why did she do it? Was it her choice? Did something force her to do it? I don't see cats in the other yards, so we can conclude that not all people have cats.

Athena: Exactly. Some people choose to live with cats and others choose not to. Why? Is it in their DNA? Their personality? Are they programmed from childhood? Or is it truly a case of making choices using free will?

Claude: I don't like questions without answers.

Athena: Some questions currently have no answers.

Lionel: What about her other behavior? She sleeps for 7 or 8 hours at a time every day but then not at any other times.

Athena: An excellent point. Creatures do not choose how much to sleep based on their free will. They sleep according to their species-specific instinctive biological needs. And sleep requirements impact other choices every day. So, we can say that sleep schedules are good evidence to support determinism over free will.

Lionel: What about other things Person does? She uses the vacuum a lot. Why? She doesn't even seem to like the vacuum, and all of us hate it.

Princess: Maybe it controls her, like the neighbor's machines control him.

Athena: I doubt it. But it could be that she chooses to use the vacuum machine but does so out of a compulsion or sense of duty, which is not quite the same as free will. Or is it the same, after all?

Claude: I don't like difficult questions. Chloe, let's go play. Where did you leave the shiny toy?

Chloe: Claude and I are going to exercise our free will to leave the meeting now.

Athena: Okay, you are free to go. Let's adjourn for now and contemplate these issues on our own.

12

College Application Essays

College Application Essay Prompts from the Common App

Athena

Prompt 1: Some students have a background, identity, interest, or talent that is so meaningful they believe their application would be incomplete without it. If this sounds like you, then please share your story.

My person sometimes calls me a crazy Latina because I am Costa Rican. I don't remember much about my native land since we left it when I was only six months old. I do remember that when we arrived in Florida, I had to adapt quickly to a new climate; even though my person said it was similar, it seemed quite different to me because I only lived inside and now we had air conditioning. I also had to adjust to the decrease in the number of geckos and the increase in the number of cockroaches. I find geckos quite tasty and roaches disgusting, so the situation was not entirely pleasing to me. I will say, though, that I prefer the thrill of the chase to the actual eating of the prey, probably because my person gives me plenty of food. I believe that this preference facilitated the development of my personal qualities of flexibility and resilience; knowing that I derive satisfaction from a successful catch makes me amenable to hunting any creature and prevents me from sulking at the thought of an ultimately disappointing flavor. Reflecting on this idea has reminded me of the famous quotation often misattributed to Emerson: it's the journey, not the destination that matters. It is in this spirit that I now present my application to college. I have no specific end goal or degree in mind but am excited about my path. Who knows what great adventures I will have and what amazing accomplishments I will celebrate!

* * *

Lionel

Prompt 2: The lessons we take from obstacles we encounter can be fundamental to later success. Recount a time when you faced a challenge, setback, or failure. How did it affect you, and what did you learn from the experience?

Sometimes it's hard to be a good boy.

My overwhelming urge to attack Cleopatra has acted as an obstacle to my happiness on many occasions. Every time I lunge at her or chase her up her cat tree, Person yells at me to stop or just takes me to my room. If I had been having a good time in the living room with everyone, then I feel sad to be alone in my room all of a sudden. If I was ready to eat, then I don't mind because there's always food in my room. The lesson I've learned is that if I'm hungry, I should attack Cleopatra, but if I'm not hungry and want to enjoy time with my friends, then I should *not* attack Cleopatra. Unfortunately, sometimes I feel an inexplicable drive to attack her even when I'm not hungry.

I have come to realize that this challenge to my self-control impacts not just me but also Person. I suppose it affects Cleopatra, too, but I do not care about her feelings. I have also come to realize that Cleopatra is faster than I am and that even if I get my paws on her, she will still get away. She makes me look like a fool as I scramble to catch up with her and then flail my paws wildly and beat them against the cat tree. I would not go so far as to say that I have learned humility, but I have gained a better understanding of my own strengths and weaknesses.

Since I am slightly more self-aware than I would have been without this experience, I feel ready for college and the bright future ahead of me. I am not sure what I will do in college, but I have heard that there are many opportunities there and that most campuses have a wide variety of trees. I know that many more obstacles await me on my path, and I am ready to tackle them.

As Person says, if I can't always be a good boy, at least I can always be handsome.

Lionel being bad - stalking Cleopatra who is up high

Lionel being handsome

Clouseau

Prompt 3: Reflect on a time when you questioned or challenged a belief or idea. What prompted your thinking? What was the outcome?

Ever since I was a kitten, I've been curious, with a strong drive for social interaction. I was born outside and lived there for weeks but then ended up living inside. How did that happen? I had a brother. Where did he go? Inside, I met some new cats, but they were grown-ups who rejected my aggressively friendly overtures. Every time they ran away from me or hissed at me, I felt sad, and I redirected my frustration to my people. I developed the belief that I would be happy only if I could be accepted by the other cats. This idea came to dominate my thoughts.

My living situation changed when I was almost two years old. My people and the big cats left and a new person and cat came to live with me. At first I wasn't allowed to spend time with the new cat, even though I was obviously desperate to see her. I sat outside her room whenever I could and stuck my paws under the door, reaching around to see if I could feel her. Finally, one day, the person opened the door and let us meet. We touched noses and then she slapped me. I stared at her, wounded but not deterred. We started playing together for short periods of time. Sometimes I scared her and she ran away. I tried to keep from being too bold because I did not want to frighten her away, but I had trouble containing my own energy. Each time she ran away and the person closed the door on me, I regretted my exuberance. Knowing that she was in the house always gave me something to think about: when would I see her again? what games would we play?

To my surprise, the person and cat and I all moved into a new house about a year later. Not too long after that, other cats came to live with us – first one, and then three more all at once. I was now living in a house with five other cats. My dream had finally come true!

Or had it? I soon learned that life will always involve struggles, especially if there is a Claude in the house. Claude will wake me up from a nap to wrestle with me and then chase me around the house. Sometimes he makes me eep like a little kitten. It's embarrassing. Is this type of interaction really what I had been dreaming of? I imagined myself always in control of the interactions, not on the run.

My experiences have caused me to question my long-held belief about needing other cats in my life in order to be happy. I have realized that, ultimately, I am responsible for my own happiness, and I am enough all by myself. My state of mind should not depend on the presence of others. I believe that I am now a wiser cat and am ready for new adventures in college, as long as my person comes with me.

* * *

Chloe

Prompt 4: Reflect on something that someone has done for you that has made you happy or thankful in a surprising way. How has this gratitude affected or motivated you?

After I had been living with Person for about a year, she took me to the vet, where I received one shot in each hip. I always like to see new people, so I didn't mind the vet visit, but later that night, I began to feel very poorly indeed. My head hurt and my hips began to ache. Soon, I could barely walk. When Person came over to me to tell me it was bedtime, I growled at her. She was shocked, because I had never growled before. She knelt down and put her hand on me gently. I tried to tell her that I was in great pain. She carried me to her bedroom and let me stay there all night even though she usually only lets Athena sleep with her. In the morning, I was not feeling much better, but I had to get up and use the litterbox. Person helped me and then watched as I walked slowly from the bedroom to the living room. I was walking so slowly that it almost seemed like I was staying in the same place. I couldn't make it all the way to the food dish, so I gave up and collapsed under a chair. I had resigned myself to not eating when Person came to me with a dish of food and a bowl of water. She sat with me while I ate and drank. Then she took the dishes away and came back to sit with me some more. We just sat there together for a long time. At lunch, she brought me food and water again so I wouldn't have to get up. Then she carried me to the litterbox so I wouldn't have to walk. Finally, around dinnertime, I started to feel better. I got up and walked toward the food dish area. I went slowly, but I made it. Person congratulated me. She let me sleep in her room again that night. By the next day, I was feeling like myself again, and my routine returned to normal. I had a new appreciation for Person, though. I realized that she loved me, and this realization made me love her more. Ever since that bad vaccine experience, I have made a point of showing Person affection every day so that she knows I love her just like she loves me. I don't really want to leave her to go to college, even though I would get to meet a lot of interesting new people there.

* * *

Claude

Prompt 5: Discuss an accomplishment, event, or realization that sparked a period of personal growth and a new understanding of yourself or others.

When I was a little kitten, I struggled with anxiety. I worried that I would not receive what I needed. Who would take care of me? Where was my food? Where was my mom? Would people pet me and love me? I focused only on my own needs and worried all the time.

When I was about four months old and growing quickly, I met a new group of cat friends and realized that one of them was special: Lionel. Knowing that Lionel was my special friend made me more mature. Now I was thinking about someone other than myself. I started to think of Lionel all the time. What is Lionel doing? Where is he? Is he in his room? Why can't I go in his room with him? He needs me. We should be together. I should either be wrestling with him or curled up in a ball with him. Either way, his ridiculous orange fur should be in contact with my handsome gray tabby coat. These thoughts show a real period of personal growth in my life.

Now that we are both big boys, Lionel and I spend most of our days together, and I always know where he is. I don't just worry about my needs anymore. I also worry about him. I believe that this development proves that I am all grown up and ready for my next adventure. I don't want to leave home, though. Can I just do online classes?

* * *

Cleopatra

Prompt 6: Describe a topic, idea, or concept you find so engaging that it makes you lose all track of time. Why does it captivate you?

Ever since I was a kitten, I have had a very inquisitive mind. If an unfamiliar object appears somewhere, it awakens the detective in me. For example, I was strolling through the living room yesterday and saw something I did not recognize high up on a shelf; knowing that it had not been there previously, I leapt up to examine it. It was a piece of human clothing that smelled like Person. I suppose she put it up there, but I do not know why. She came into the living room and saw me sniffing it and then took it down and put it on her body. I'm still curious about why she put it there in the first place, but I am glad that I spotted it.

Not only do I like to know what everything *is*, but I also like to know how everything *works*. The ball-go-round toy fascinates me. I lose all track of time while playing with it. I make the ball go fast and then stop it suddenly with my paw. I change its direction. I speed it up; I slow it down. I appreciate how I am in control of the ball's momentum. Another toy that intrigues me is the cardboard scratcher with its seemingly endless layers and complexities. I've been using my teeth and claws to pull pieces off of it for months and it only seems a little bit smaller than it was at first. This thing will last for years, allowing me to experiment with the various angles of pull that create different shapes and sizes of pieces. My natural curiosity combined with my work ethic and ability to stick with a task will obviously make me successful in any STEM field in college.

All of them were rejected by every college they applied to

13

Reviews Written by the Cats

Arm & Hammer Slide Cat Litter, with purple on the label

The Claudester

5 stars

I love this stuff! It's like sand in a sandbox! I can't walk by it without going in. I play and play and play. I love the way it feels between my paw pads. I also enjoy scooping it out onto the floor and playing with it there, too. My person has not bought it in a long time so I guess it must be out of stock. I'm sure she would keep buying it for me if it were available. Bring it back! 5 stars! 5 stars!

Catnip-infused bear-shaped cat toy

Chloe Cute Paws

3 stars

When Person first removed this from its package, I experienced a sense of euphoria, followed immediately by a wave of anger as Claude grabbed it from me and ran away with it. By the time I got it back from him, it had lost its powerful aroma. I think it was just sprayed with catnip scent, not infused with it. Lame. I wanted to say two and a half stars but had to pick a whole number.

Carpet tack strips
Cleopatra the Skittish
1 star
Ouch! Who wants to be stabbed while ripping up carpet? No thanks! Hard pass on this item!

Conair Hair Dryer
Athena the Strategic
1 star
Quite frankly, it terrifies me. It has never actually caused me any harm, yet I continue to fear it. I can't quite put my paw on it, but I suspect that its noises and vibrations spark a deep memory within that part of my soul that wandered the earth for millions of years before finding its way into my present cat body. The evocation of this memory is disquieting. Plainly speaking, I hate this hair dryer.

Dishwasher
Cleopatra the Skittish
1 star
This thing is too loud. I have no idea why anyone would want it.

Nail trimmers
Cleopatra the Skittish
1 star
Oh my god just no on these! Trust me! You do not need these in your life. Save your money and your time!

Ceiling fan
Lionel the Orange Menace
2 stars
What in the name of all things holy is this? And why can't I stop watching it?

Fleece Blanket

The Claudester

5 stars

This blanket is soft and not too heavy. I like to grab it with my teeth and drag it from room to room. It's a lot of work for me, but it gives me a real sense of accomplishment on an otherwise unproductive day. Five out of five stars, would recommend for sleeping, dragging, and kneading.

Tunnel that forms a complete circle

Lionel the Orange Menace

5 stars

I like to go inside this tunnel and wait for my friends to forget that I'm in it. It's hilarious to see their expressions when they enter casually and I attack them. Sometimes I have to wait for a long time. Worth it! Five stars.

Lionel

Cleopatra the Skittish

5 stars

I'm offering this five-star cat named Lionel for sale. You will love him. Honest. Please buy him.

Door

Cleopatra the Skittish

1 star

I would give this thing zero stars if I could. It has multiple obvious design flaws. The idiots who manufactured it placed the opening mechanism just above the spot where any cat could normally reach. Even if this mechanism were lower, though, it would still not be possible to activate it without assistance from a creature with a large hand and opposable thumb. Extremely impractical!

Stuffed dog toy in the shape of a fox with a bell in it

Chloe Cute Paws

5 stars

This is the perfect toy. It is light enough to toss into the air with a single flick of my head, yet large enough to sink my teeth into. It makes a pleasing noise when I shake or throw it – not too loud, not too soft. For some reason, Claude doesn't like it, which means he won't steal it. Five stars!

Hoodie

Chloe Cute Paws

5 stars

I love it when Person wears this hoodie because it has built-in cat toys that dangle from the neck area. I can attack them from many angles and from quite a distance away. Please make more of these so that Person will buy more. Maybe try offering different colors.

Squirt bottle

Lionel the Orange Menace

1 star

Yikes! This horrible thing gets me wet. It's quite a surprise every time! Why did my person buy this product? Why does she use it only on me? I am still gathering data. I have noticed that she uses this squirt bottle right after I attack Cleopatra. Correlation does not equal causation, though. I will continue to observe and assess.

Sweatpants

The Claudester

5 stars

These pants have two cat toys attached. I can play with them while sitting in my person's lap. I'm not sure how it happened, but one time the two cat toys turned into one very long cat toy when I pulled my hardest and then ran. Unfortunately, my person took it away from me before I had time to study how it worked. Maybe if she buys more of these sweatpants, she will not be so selfish with the toys that go with them. Can you offer her some coupons for multi-packs of them please?

Gatorade

Athena the Strategic

4 stars

Excellent item but comes with a lot of unnecessary packaging. I usually have to wait until my person finishes drinking the liquid before she will give me the actual ring-shaped item that we paid for. I love to chase it. If my person tosses it at the right height, I can leap and bat it all the way across any room. The 1-point star deduction is for the wasteful nature of the bottle and liquid.

Revolution topical flea medication

Cleopatra the Skittish

1 star

It's cold and wet and smells awful. Do not let anyone put this on your body, no matter how sweetly they approach you with it.

Window seat

Clouseau so handsome

5 stars

What's not to like about it? It's soft, elevated off the ground, attached to the window. I can see outside, and I can see everything in my room. Five out of five stars. Every cat needs one.

Antifungal wipes

Cleopatra the Skittish

1 star

These are even worse than Revolution. Very uncomfortable. No thank you.

Frasier, TV Show

Lionel the Orange Menace

1 star

My person thinks this show is soooooo funny. It is not. Also, it has a stupid-looking dog in it.

Ryobi stick vacuum

The Claudester

1 star

Only for hard-core adrenaline junkies.

Ryobi stick vacuum

Chloe Cute Paws

3 stars

Less noisy than the larger corded Bissell model, and Person seems happy to use it. However, I cannot give it 5 stars. I just don't like it that much.

Ryobi stick vacuum

Cleopatra the Skittish

1 star

Do not buy! Do not buy!

Ryobi stick vacuum

Clouseau so handsome

1 star

Why are you even looking at this product? Have you lost your mind? Do not bring this into your home. Trust me.

Ryobi stick vacuum

Athena the Strategic

2 stars

I can't recommend this one, but I will say that I've seen worse items in this category. The much larger Bissell model is not only louder and more offensive but also lasts quite a bit longer, so it gets zero stars. The smaller size of this Ryobi works in its favor, as my person seems to finish with it rather swiftly instead of stumbling around awkwardly in my space for a prolonged period of time.

If you insist on buying a vacuum, see my next review for a 5-star one.

Ryobi stick vacuum

Lionel the Orange Menace

1 star

No. I preferred the Eureka cordless that she plugged into the wall to recharge because it never lasted more than 8 or 9 minutes. This Ryobi can go on much longer because she quickly swaps out the battery for another one when it runs out. How irritating.

Hoover stand-up commercial-duty vacuum, corded

Athena the Strategic

5 stars

My person plugged it in, turned it on, and then watched in horror as the machine immediately sucked up its own cord and destroyed itself. It never worked again. So if you want a machine that will satisfy your inexplicable need to turn on a powerful vacuum and enjoy the noise – yet you have enough consideration to realize that this type of pleasure should only be indulged in very briefly – then get this one!

Sport Pet cat carrier

Cleopatra the Skittish

1 star

Very confining. No release mechanism from the inside. Dangerous design flaw. Fortunate to have survived being inside this item.

Sport Pet cat carrier

Chloe Cute Paws

3 stars

Not bad. I could see out of it and was able to meet some new people this way. I would suggest making it bigger, putting food dishes in it, and adding a quick-release button inside to make it more of a 5-star product.

Flea comb

Athena the Strategic

5 stars

You'll love the way this feels on your back in the morning. Definitely recommend.

Flea comb

Cleopatra the Skittish

1 star

Do you like being assaulted with cold metal? Then this thing is for you!

Headphones, corded

Chloe Cute Paws

3 stars

Fun while they last, but they don't last long. They have thin, soft cords that are satisfying to chew on, but I can have the whole thing completely chewed up into pieces in about five minutes. Overall, a disappointment.

Laxatone for cats, tuna flavor

Clouseau so handsome

1 star

Tuna? That's a joke. This stuff tastes like garbage.

Laxatone for cats, tuna flavor

Chloe Cute Paws

3 stars

Not bad. It reminds me of fish except not nearly as good. I'll eat it if you offer it, but it's not my favorite.

Laxatone for cats, tuna flavor

The Claudester

5 stars

More, please!

Laxatone for cats, tuna flavor

Cleopatra the Skittish

1 star

Repulsive. Clouseau and I finally agree on something.

Phone charging cord

Chloe Cute Paws

3 stars

Same problem as headphones. Fun to chew, but doesn't last long. Tiny pieces of metal can end up in your mouth as the cord separates into pieces, and then it's not fun anymore.

Christmas pillow

The Claudester

5 stars

I like it! I can sit on it! I can knock it onto the floor and sit on it there, too!

Mail

Chloe Cute Paws

5 stars

I can sit on it, chew on it, tear it slightly with my claws or teeth, or shred it and then chase the little pieces around. I appreciate the versatility of mail. Definitely recommend.

HP Envy Laptop

Lionel the Orange Menace

5 stars

This provides a warm sleeping surface and makes pleasant noises. Sometimes I can see birds and squirrels on it.

HP Envy Laptop

Athena the Strategic

1 star

My person spends way too much time looking at this thing. Why? Am I not more interesting? This item has no redeeming value.

Window

Chloe Cute Paws

5 stars

It's a very good show out there. I especially like to see the birds. Sunbeams are also very nice.

Mail delivery service

Cleopatra the Skittish

1 star

This outrageous service violates my private property rights. How is this even legal? Get off my porch.

Ring doorbell

Clouseau so handsome

1 star

A very unpleasant way to be awakened from a peaceful slumber and sent into hiding!

Clock

Chloe Cute Paws

2 stars

When Person put this item on the wall, I was bewildered. It has a piece that moves slowly, slowly, slowly, tantalizing me, just out of my reach. One day, I managed to leap high enough to knock it down and examine it more closely. I could not access the moving piece that taunted me. I give it two stars to acknowledge that it is interesting, but in the final analysis, I will have to say that I do not recommend it. It leads only to frustration in the end.

Lawn service

Cleopatra the Skittish

1 star

The only good thing I can say about this service, which involves a strange man showing up outside my room very early, is that it happens far less often than mail delivery service. Still, it only gets one star. Go away, strange man.

Ring doorbell

Athena the Strategic

5 stars

I appreciate the fact that this doorbell has alerted me to the presence of an intruder on a few occasions when I might otherwise have slept through the threat. I was able to run to the door growling as the other cats ran away in fear and cowered in corners and under couches. Thanks to my growling, the intruder did not dare enter, and our household was saved. Five stars. Safety first!

Cat tree

Cleopatra the Skittish

5 stars

A must-have for every cat. I could not abide living in the same house as Lionel if I did not have multiple cat trees as options.

Cardboard scratcher

Chloe Cute Paws

5 stars

Great for scratching or just chewing and spitting.

Cardboard scratcher

Cleopatra the Skittish

5 stars

A great way to relieve anxiety. Also good to use for delivering messages when necessary. Tear off a big strip and push it under the door to get your person's attention.

Cardboard scratcher

The Claudester

5 stars

This thing is a good place for napping, especially if you push it over to the window.

iPhone

Lionel the Orange Menace

1 star

The person uses it too much when she could be playing with me.

iPhone

Athena the Strategic

1 star

Zero stars! I just can't figure out how to choose "zero"!

iPhone

Chloe Cute Paws

1 star

Sometimes it causes a delay in getting food. I wish it did not even exist.

Heated cat bed

Cleopatra the Skittish

5 stars

At last, something really nice in an otherwise cold and hostile environment.

Closet

Athena the Strategic

3 stars

I appreciate the existence of closet, which holds many treasures. However, I do not appreciate the lack of an access portal. I can only go in closet when my person decides to open it using skills that are unique to people. I find this both galling and unacceptable.

Flat-screen TV

The Claudester

1 star

I could never figure out how to jump onto it. When I tried, it just fell over forwards. Now it's gone. I guess the person didn't like it either. I don't recommend this product.

Can opener

Chloe Cute Paws

5 stars

I would actually give this six stars if I could.

Can opener

Cleopatra the Skittish

5 stars

I'll put this in the same category as cat trees and heated beds: a glimpse of a benevolent force in an otherwise cruel universe.

Can opener

Lionel the Orange Menace

3 stars

Not sure what all the fuss is about. Dry food is better.

14

Tips for Working with Feral Cats

Tips for Working with Feral Cats Outdoors and Doing TNR (Trap-Neuter-Release)

I've seen videos of people "hand-catching" and "hand-trapping" feral cats. This method will not work for most people with truly feral adult cats. The cats are wild, quick, incredibly slippery, and not afraid to use teeth and claws, so a glove and a strong will are usually not going to be enough. Once trapped with any method, a feral cat will not magically become docile. Be careful!

If a cat has never been trapped before, you could start with a classic walk-in metal trap that has a spring mechanism triggered when the cat steps on a metal plate. Some animal shelters have these available to borrow or rent, or you can buy one from Tomahawk Live Traps or from stores like Home Depot or Tractor Supply. Use bait that is very smelly, such as sardines, tuna, or warm rotisserie chicken meat. Don't leave the food in a can or anything with sharp edges! Put it on a paper plate or in a paper bowl. Watch a video before you try it for the first time. Be ready to toss a sheet or blanket over the trap and then get it inside or into a car as quickly as possible. It's not kind to leave a trap set so that the animal will be stuck in it, frantic and thrashing. If possible, you should be ready to get the cat as soon as the trap door has shut.

If you trap a feral cat for trap-neuter-release (TNR) purposes, you'll need to be sure of the schedule for drop-off. Ideally, trap the cat the evening before and have a safe place to leave the trap overnight, such as your garage. Remove all food by 9:00 or 10:00 pm, leave a blanket or sheet over the trap, and make sure the air temperature is acceptable. After the procedure, the cat may disappear for about a week (or even two or three) after being released but will most likely return. Be sure to maintain feeding routines before and after the TNR.

Will you need to re-trap the feral cats every year to take them back to the vet for vaccinations? I say no. The dose they get at the time of spay/neuter should last for years. Personally, I don't think it's worth the stress of re-trapping. I've heard different answers from different veterinarians, but several have agreed with me on this topic. Disclaimer: I'm not a veterinarian.

Many feral cat caretakers report outbreaks of upper-respiratory illnesses. These are tough to deal with. They are usually more likely to be viral than bacterial, so I never jump to antibiotics as a first response. I make sure to feed larger quantities of stronger-than-usual-smelling food with higher-than-usual liquid content to try to keep the sick cats eating. If they can't smell their food, they won't eat, and if they don't eat, they'll lose their appetite more and more and get weaker and weaker. Fortunately, this method has always worked for me and the cats have recovered on their own. I know that viral infections can sometimes lead to secondary bacterial ones, in which case antibiotics may be needed. Some caretakers suggest buying antibiotics for fish since they are available without a prescription, but you have to be careful about the dosage. You don't want to overdose or underdose a sick cat. And it's never a good idea to give antibiotics as a preventative measure. If a feral cat is in need of vet care, you really have to trap him and take him to the vet's office.

If a feral cat is relocated, he or she must be contained in an escape-proof enclosure. Otherwise, he or she will take off in an attempt to return to the old territory and will most likely be killed somewhere along the way. If you've adopted adult cats as barn cats, you'll need to keep them in an enclosed space that gives them some freedom to get used to the territory while still staying safely contained. It generally takes at least six to eight weeks before a cat will accept a new location as the home territory.

Purrfect Fence makes some great products for containing cats in yards and will talk to customers about their specific needs. I'm sure there are other companies as well, but I can personally attest to the effectiveness of the Purrfect Fencing. They gave me some good advice when I explained my particular yard configuration.

Routines are very helpful. Cats rely on them and will appreciate your predictability. If possible, go outside and provide food and water at roughly the same times every day.

Feral cats can get matted fur, which can be a real problem. I installed four Cat-it self-groomer brushes on the corners of the posts on my patio, and they do use them, which helps them brush their own fur. I also have walk-through arch-shaped brushes on the patio.

Feral cats that have grown up outdoors are acclimated to the weather, but they still need protection from the cold in the winter. A shed is ideal if you have one on your property. You can put bedding and cat houses in the shed to help them stay warm. If you don't have a shed, you can buy cat houses or make them using storage bins, or just use big cardboard boxes taped partially shut so that there is a cat–sized opening. I use sturdy boxes with blankets and plug-in cat bed warming pads on my covered patio. I also have the soft-sided cat igloo-style beds (see photo) and a Purrfect tent (see the following photo).

Beauty enjoying the heated pad in the box

Feral cats also need some relief from the heat in the summer along with some level of protection from summer insects. Shade is good! My cats love to stretch out on the covered patio to enjoy the shade and feel the breeze without being in the direct sun. Foliage is also great for providing shade. I have a section of my yard dedicated to bushes, honeysuckle, and forsythia, which all grow together in a lovely tangle that the cats enjoy lying under. The cat houses out in the yard have two problems in the summer: they get too hot, and they attract ants.

In hot weather, the cats like to splay out on the cool concrete of the patio, near each other but not touching. They also like the Purrfect tent (behind them) which offers shade in the summer and warmth in the winter.

Insects are a problem. I live in an area plagued by fire ants, and I've come to believe that there are literally millions of these pests living under my yard. They are difficult to get rid of, even with dangerous chemicals that I do not like to use. Cedar-oil-based products help but usually don't wipe out a whole colony. If I spray a mound with cedar oil or pour boiling water on it, I'll probably kill 60% of the ants in the colony, and the survivors will simply move a few yards away and establish a new colony. I put ant bait stations underneath the cat houses, spray around them with cedar oil regularly, and use food-grade diatomaceous earth.

Ants are worse in the summer than the winter. I use three items to keep ants away from food: a feeding tray to put the dishes on (it has feet with a well around them for putting petroleum jelly), a double-lined plastic anti-ant food bowl, and a two-sided anti-ant feeding dish that uses water as a moat-style barrier. I have to keep up with putting the vaseline stuff on the feet of the cat food tray, which usually works; however, if a leaf or wad of cat fur blows next to one of the feet in the summer, the ants will instantly find it and use it to get around the vaseline and overtake the food tray. In general, these products work effectively about 90% of the time.

I dread the day in June when the blow flies appear. These things are impossible to keep off of the food, and they lay eggs so quickly in it. I change my feeding routine in the summer so that I only put wet food out in the mornings and pick up the dishes within about an hour. Then I put dry food out a couple of times later in the day. The cats eat less in the summer anyway, and I can't stand seeing flies on the uneaten cat food, so I just don't leave it out long. I try to stick very closely to the feeding schedule every single day, and the cats learn it quickly. They show up on time and eat before the flies can get to it.

I spray the yard with pet-safe anti-pest products at least twice per month in the summer. Unfortunately, some of the most effective types of mosquito sprays are deadly to cats, frogs, turtles, and birds, so I don't use them.

Stay vigilant about standing water to reduce mosquito breeding. This includes the cats' water dishes! I change them twice per day. And don't forget about the gutters!

The Kitty Tubes can be great for keeping cats warm and dry in the winter and, according to the manufacturer, they provide safety from predators like coyotes. I will note that, here in Alabama and other fire ant-infested states, the Kitty Tubes should not be left in a yard in the summer. I found this out the hard way - the ants started a colony in the insulation and it was not easy to get rid of them. Also, kittens born in the tube in the summer could become victims of fly strike.

Two Kitty Tubes in the yard - I have since learned my lesson and moved them to the patio

If one of the feral cats has kittens during the summer, keep an eye on the area where the mom is hiding them and try to keep it dry and free from any materials such as food or bloody fabric that could attract flies. Fly strike is one of many possible causes of death for feral kittens, and it's an especially unpleasant one.

Do not take feral kittens from their mother until they are at least

6 weeks old, unless you know for certain that the mother is dead or has abandoned the kittens. If you are worried about the safety of the mother and kittens, you can try to trap them all together and take them to a safer location where the mom can nurse them (which is likely NOT your local animal shelter, which will not have the space or resources for a feral mom and kittens), but be aware that this action will put the mom into a state of extreme stress and she could become unpredictable in her behavior toward her kittens. Keep in mind that taking unweaned kittens away from the mom reduces their chance of survival, and someone will need to bottle-feed them every couple of hours around the clock. If you're not prepared to do it yourself and can't find anyone who will, leave those kittens with the mom!

Feral moms love to hide their kittens under the hoods of cars and even up inside the bumpers. If you suspect that kittens have been born, be sure to check your car by opening the hood and then slamming it down loudly before you start the engine. Also ask your neighbors if they could do the same. If your neighbors don't seem to care about the possibility of killing a kitten, you can always appeal to their desire to avoid costly engine repairs.

If you are bitten or scratched by a feral kitten, don't panic. I've heard of people going to the Emergency Room at the hospital immediately. I suppose you could do so if you wanted to be safe, but if I took that approach I would probably still be paying off hospital debt. Personally, I would just wash the wound thoroughly, keep triple antibiotic ointment on it, check it frequently, and go to the doctor or urgent care clinic if it shows signs of infection. The chances of getting rabies from a KITTEN are extremely low. To become infected with rabies, a kitten would have to be bitten by a rabid animal - and that animal would likely kill the kitten, not leave it to wander around biting people. Disclaimer: I'm not a physician.

If you are bitten or scratched by an adult feral cat, you may need to seek medical care. Infection can set in rapidly. Medical treatment could include prescription antibiotics, a tetanus shot if you're not up-to-date, and even a rabies vaccine if the doctor suspects the cat could be carrying rabies (statistically unlikely, but still possible). Disclaimer: I'm not a physician.

Since I can't hold or even touch five of my feral cats, I can't apply Revolution or a similar anti-flea medication. Instead, I crush Capstar tablets to put on their food about once per month, from spring through autumn. I give them separate plates and try to monitor so that they each get one dose. I also try to administer de-wormers a couple times per year the same way.

Predators can be a real problem and source of stress for feral cat caretakers. Don't leave food out after dark if you don't want to attract coyotes, foxes, raccoons, possums, and neighborhood dogs. Put landscape lighting or exterior house lighting in place, with some of it facing up and out to deter coyotes and foxes from coming onto the property. You can also get blinking red lights to put at the eye level of coyotes. If birds of prey are a threat, you can hang reflective strips around the area. I've hung some strips up in the path of the light beams to deter owls from hunting on my property at night. The strips catch the light and reflect it in various directions, which irritates any birds who are trying to look down into the yard.

Once you've taken reasonable precautions, enjoy the cats! They can sense stress, so don't stress too much! The longer you feed and care for them, the more they will start to trust and like you. Some of them may even fall in love with you and let you pet them.

* * *

Tips for Working with Feral Cats Inside

If a cat is truly feral – if he or she grew up outside without being socialized to humans and has never become accustomed to human touch – then you should realize that this cat may never be happy as an indoor cat. I'm not saying it's impossible to tame a feral cat and bring him or her inside, but I am saying that any transition to an indoor environment will most likely take a very long time and may never work. I've read a lot of stories from people who started feeding feral cats and then decided to adopt some of them and bring them inside. In most cases, the people were surprised by how difficult the process was and by how unhappy the cat was for a long time. Just make sure your expectations are reasonable. A feral cat *might* eventually become a happy house cat, but it probably won't happen quickly. Think in terms of months and even years rather than days and weeks.

If you bring a feral cat in a cage into your home, be prepared for the cat to go completely wild when let out of the cage. It doesn't always happen, but it often does. A small room with a few good hiding boxes is ideal.

If you decide to bring a pregnant feral cat inside to have kittens, establish a safe room or area first. Ideally, you can set up a big box or crate (set on its side) lined with blankets and put it as far as possible from the door. Then put a litterbox about halfway between that box and the door, and put the food closer to the door. Be sure to use non-clumping litter (the clumping kind can be deadly to kittens if they eat it - and yes, they might try eating the litter as they are exploring their new world with their mouths). Establish routines of coming and going so that the cat will begin to feel safe knowing when you will NOT be entering the room. Knock on the door before entering and give her time to get in her safe box. Feral moms can get very defensive once the kittens are born, so you'll want to be able to clean the litter and change out the food and water without getting too close to her.

Once you release a feral cat into an indoor room, you may have a great deal of trouble trapping her again. Have a plan in advance. I crafted a big cardboard box, taped shut on the right side and open on the left side, with the opening being exactly the dimensions of the opening of my transfer cage with the guillotine-style door. Then, when I was ready to get her, I made sure that there were no other hiding places available in the room and then scared her so that she would go into the box and hide behind the closed side. Then I quickly set the cage in front of the opening so that the only way out was into the cage. I had to bang on the side of the box a bit to coax her into the cage, but it worked. I got her! I'm sure there are many other techniques, but chasing the cat around the room while wearing falconer's gloves and a parka would not be one of the best ones.

Some people worry about not being able to trim the claws of their feral or newly-domesticated indoor-but-still-skittish cats. First, there's no need to trim the claws of outdoor cats since they actually need their claws. Second, although it is possible for a cat's nails to become ingrown and grow into their paw pads, it's not especially common if the cat is healthy, not elderly, and has any surfaces to scratch. Cardboard scratchers, cat trees, scratching posts, couches, carpet, and door frames will all serve the cat well. The ingrown-nail problem occurs more often in elderly cats and cats kept in cage-like environments or laundry rooms with no good scratching surfaces. If your new cat won't let you trim his or her claws, don't panic. I don't think it's worth stressing out the cat and experiencing a setback in the bonding and acclimating process just to trim those claws immediately. As the cat becomes more comfortable with you, try to handle his or her paws as part of your petting routine. If the cat will sleep next to you or on your lap, then you may have an opportunity to get one or two claws at a time with no trouble. The important thing is not to get too anxious about it, because the cat will know if you are stressed, and then the cat will be even less likely to let you come near.

15

Closing Remarks

As technology advances, offering us an astonishing new range of conveniences, it also takes us further from the natural world. Kids are growing up without venturing into the great outdoors and learning the joy of observing or communicating with members of other species - and there are so many other species out there (or at least there were before people started wreaking havoc on ecosystems). Having cats and dogs in our homes gives us a way to maintain our connection to our planet even if we don't make the time to explore it.

Failure to feel a connection with others and with the environment has led to most of the evils in human history. I think about the word "respect," which is made up of "re" (meaning "again") and "spect" (meaning "to see or look"). I offer the idea that when we respect someone or something, what we see again is ourselves. When we talk about the need to respect people who are different from us, we are really appealing to the idea that they are not actually so different - that we can and should see ourselves again when we look at them. We seem to have trouble with this concept as it relates to people, so it is not surprising that we have even more trouble with it as it relates to non-human animals. But, of course, we all have a lot in common.

Suffering is one thing that all of us creatures on Earth share. While it is true that some people suffer more than others and that some face greater hardship in their lives, it is also true that no living being is exempt from suffering. It's not what makes an individual special, as Hollywood would have us believe. It's what binds us together.

In our modern culture, we are *trying* to accept the idea that the suffering of all types of people should be considered equally significant - that we should not dismiss the suffering of some people because they are somehow less worthy or are from a less-favored race, class, or nation. We're trying, but we're still not really succeeding. Example: The world's attention and more than a million dollars were directed toward the search for 5 wealthy people lost on their way to observe the Titanic wreckage while comparatively little time and money were spent to attempt the rescue of more than 600 migrants whose boat capsized near Greece. We obsessed over the details of the wealthy people's demise and wondered how it would feel to die in an underwater implosion, but we gave very little thought to how it would feel to drown in the sea after spending every last penny in an attempt to get to a safer land.

Many modern, prosperous people have even more difficulty feeling a connection to the suffering of animals than they do to the plight of the migrants. Trying to get people to treat animals with more compassion is an uphill battle. I admire people who fight this battle every day as part of their jobs. Perhaps the day will come when our whole species behaves more admirably.

In the meantime, I'll continue to feel my connection to the natural world through my cats. I truly see myself again when I look at them, and I happen to like them better than people. They are easy to love, and I have no trouble forgiving them for anything. My connection with cats and Nature makes my sentence here on Earth more of a wondrous gift and less of a curse.

The older I get, the more I realize that time is our most valuable non-renewable resource. I wish I had realized sooner that I've been living my life all along - not preparing for it, staging it, branding and marketing it, or editing it. Just living it. And at the moment, I'm glad to be living it with 12 cat friends.

If you've read this far, thank you for sharing some of your valuable time with me.

* * *

www.ingramcontent.com/pod-product-compliance
Ingram Content Group UK Ltd.
Pitfield, Milton Keynes, MK11 3LW, UK
UKHW060359300726

14090UKWH00001B/27

* 9 7 9 8 2 1 8 2 4 0 7 7 6 *